ABCs of SEO Search Engine Optimization 101

By Roggie "Raj" Clark

Copyright

Title: ABCs Of SEO Search Engine Optimization 101
Author: Roggie "Raj" Clark

Published by Bounce Rank
Odenton, MD 21113
USA
https://www.bouncerank.com

Cover Design: Roggie Clark
Editing: Renee' Clark

ISBN: 979-8-218-19232-7

Printed in the United States of America

Disclaimer

The views and opinions expressed in this book are those of the author and do not necessarily reflect the official policy or position of any individual, company, or organization cited or referenced in the text. The author is not affiliated with any of the individuals, companies, or organizations mentioned in the text, nor does the author receive any form of compensation for citing or referencing them. Some sample scenarios in this text are fictitious. Any similarity to actual persons, living or dead, is coincidental.

The professional information (strategies, tips, and concepts) in this text is distributed on an "as is" basis, without warranty. While every precaution has been taken in the preparation of the text to ensure all information is accurate, neither the author nor the publisher shall have any liability to any person or entity with respect to any loss or damage caused or alleged to be caused directly or indirectly by the instructions contained in this text or by the computer software and hardware products described in it.

The author nor the publisher guarantees any specific results or outcomes, and the information provided in this text should not be construed as professional advice. Readers should always consult with a qualified professional before making any significant changes to their website or business.

By reading this text, you agree that the author nor the publisher is responsible for any direct, indirect, incidental, or consequential damages that may arise from the use of the information provided. You assume full responsibility for any actions taken based on the information presented in this text.

Acknowledgments

I want to thank some people near and dear to me who inspired me to write this book. The first person I'd like to acknowledge is my sister, and best friend, Reneé Clark. She is an SEO professional such as myself, my closest friend, and the most reliable person I've ever worked with.

She helped me painstakingly go through this book, page by page, to ensure that everything made sense and was written in a respectable format. So I want to thank you, Renee'; I couldn't have done it without you!

The following person I want to thank is my uncle Sean Nesbitt, who unfortunately passed away before this book came to fruition. If there's anyone in my family who would always let me know how amazing and gifted I am, it was him. And I am eternally grateful for his support.

There's one funny statement that I always remember from him, and that is, *"I don't know what it is you actually do for work, but I like it and keep doing it."* It was the unfortunate loss of him as well as his motivating words, that helped push me along to finish this book. So, thank you, Uncle Seanie, for your love, inspiration, and support.

And the last person I want to thank before this book starts is my mom. My mother helped inspire me to chase my dreams and believe in myself, even when things weren't going my way.

It's important to acknowledge these people before the book begins to give you some idea of the deeper story of this book.

Preface

The idea of writing a book about SEO arose from my desire to learn the entire topic. I spent hours reading blogs, watching videos, and taking courses to learn the basics.

But I discovered that I was consuming so much content that it was challenging to apply anything I learned. In other words, I was suffering from *"Analysis Paralysis,"* or wanting to do everything so perfectly that I did nothing at all. Maybe some of you can relate!

Despite my analysis paralysis, I began to piece together this complex topic. Then one day, I thought, "How great would it be to create a resource to help me remember and synthesize these concepts?" My desire to create an SEO resource for myself manifested into wanting to create an all-encompassing resource that could also help others.

While writing this book, I spent months acquiring resources and reviewing different perspectives on SEO. I wanted to ensure that when I gave you this book, you would receive a piece of literature that skillfully weaves together the concepts of SEO in an easy-to-understand fashion.

I hope that from reading this, you will be able to apply these ideas right away and not suffer from that sense of analysis paralysis that I felt or maybe you have experienced in the past.

It was important to share with you a deeper perspective on my overall intent for producing this piece of content.

College or University Usage

I chose to take a different approach for this book than some of the other SEO books on the market. I explained SEO in a dissertation-style format in my book, with APA references and in-text quotes.

I wrote my book in this manner because I want colleges and universities to feel comfortable utilizing this book to help their students understand the basics of SEO and how it is used in today's digital landscape. With so much information on the internet and everyone claiming to be an "expert," I felt it was imperative to write this book based on facts rather than opinions.

SEO is a booming industry with no chance of slowing down (kudos to the higher learning institutions for offering courses to teach this subject), and this book is my way of helping to make it easier.

I recommend that college deans and professors consider this book for their curriculum and as a resource for your students to use for their research. If you want to use the text for your course or have your bookstore source it for students to purchase, you can contact me directly.

Please email me at **bouncerankseo@gmail.com**. In your email, please include the following information:

- Your name
- The school you represent
- The class size you are teaching
- The length of your course (e.g. 6-week course, 12-week course, etc.)
- Any other important information I should know

My administrative assistant will email you back within 24 - 48 hours with rates, and an information sheet to use for your class.

Table of Contents

➤ **Introduction**

➤ **Chapter 1: What is SEO**

➤ **Chapter 2: What are Search Engines**

➤ **Chapter 3: Keywords**

➤ **Chapter 4: Technical SEO**

➤ **Chapter 5: HyperText Markup Language**

➤ **Chapter 6: On-Page SEO**

➤ **Chapter 7: Off-Page SEO**

➤ **Chapter 8: Key Performance Indicators**

➤ **Closing Remarks**

➤ **Glossary**

➤ **References**

Introduction

Thank you for selecting my book and reading it to advance your Search Engine Optimization (SEO) knowledge and skill. I am genuinely grateful and consider it an absolute blessing that you chose my book.

I am fully aware there are many reading materials available about SEO. At this point, it may seem nauseating to hear yet another perspective on the topic.

However, as a current professional in the field, it was imperative that I contribute to the knowledge base and provide my unique perspective.

Many SEO books instruct you on how to do SEO for a website or a blog, often with a thin promise of getting "page 1 rankings guaranteed."

But here is what makes my book different from the other SEO reading materials out there:

The *ABCs of SEO Search Engine Optimization 101* explores the subject from a historical lens and does not include any specific directions for how to perform or implement SEO.

This was purposeful, as my intention is to give you the subject in its rawest form and instead provide you with suggestions that you can use to influence and formulate your SEO strategies and tactics.

You will soon find that as you explore the topic of SEO in greater detail, the subject is constantly changing.

Tactics and strategies that may be applicable or effective today can quickly become outdated and irrelevant tomorrow.

Due to the *fluid* nature of SEO, I wrote this book in a manner that ensures that the information contained in these pages will still be relevant, or somewhat relevant, in the years to come.

My goal is for this book to be a timeless resource for you, so I have made decisions to avoid discussing specific ranking methods. Instead, I focus on explaining the fundamental concepts of SEO and guide you on how to best apply them to your unique website.

Let's shift gears and discuss how to make the best use of this book.

How to Use the Book

For first-time readers, I recommend that you read the book all the way through and try not to stress about fully comprehending each component.

As you are reading and learning about so many new ideas and concepts, it is easy to become flustered or overwhelmed. To help curve the "information overload", I highly encourage you to *take your time* and read the book thoroughly.

You may find it helpful to take notes or write down questions as you read so that you can review them later. SEO can be a rather complicated topic to learn, especially for someone who has never been exposed to basic marketing concepts. Taking notes and jotting down questions can help you process the information a little easier.

Here are some additional tips for successful reading:

- Use a highlighter to mark the chapters and sections that are most important to you.
- On your second read, look up any information you didn't understand during your first read.
- Ask questions in forums, don't be afraid to seek advice.
- Read other SEO books and articles to gain additional perspectives.

Last Thoughts

In conclusion, I aim to provide an easy-to-understand yet comprehensive explanation of SEO.

I hope this information will help you make more informed decisions about your business or website. And by doing so, you can get closer to achieving your marketing goals.

Let's segway into Chapter 1, where I will explain what SEO is and why learning it may be worth your time and effort.

Chapter 1: What is SEO

Search Engine Optimization (SEO) is a *conceptual framework* of thinking processes, tactics, and strategies used to "optimize" or improve a website to increase the likelihood that the website's content will appear in more favorable positions on search engines like Google, Bing, and Yahoo!

Let's explore the framework of SEO in greater detail.

Three Domains of SEO

The overarching concept of SEO is composed of three main components or *domains*, **Technical SEO**, **On-Page SEO**, and **Off-Page SEO.**

Here is a graphic that you can use to help you make sense of the three domains:

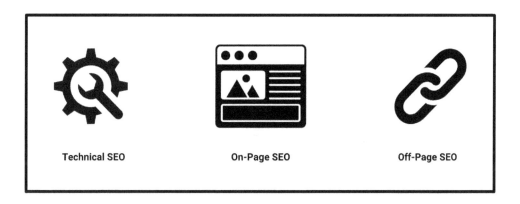

To provide more context to the graphic:

1. **Technical SEO** refers to improving the technical capabilities of a website to make it easier to use and "crawl" or be interpreted by search engines.
2. **On-Page SEO** refers to improving the information and *HTML elements* on a website to make it easier to consume for users, and easier to understand for search engines.

3. **Off-Page SEO**, also sometimes referred to as *Link-building* refers to building "backlinks" or gaining editorial votes to improve a website's notoriety and visibility.

We will explore each domain of SEO in further detail in future chapters, but for now, it is essential to know that improving elements in these three pillars are the foundation of a strong SEO strategy.

Over the following few sections, we will explore why SEO traffic is valuable and what makes it an effective way to market your website.

Why is SEO Traffic Valuable

There are many reasons why someone would perform SEO. For business owners and marketers in particular, SEO is prized because it is believed to increase the number of "qualified" website visitors - which are people most likely to purchase a company's products or services.

Search Engine Journal (2018) conducted a poll and discovered that 49% of respondents stated that SEO traffic produced a higher return on investment (ROI) than any other digital marketing channels (e.g., social media, Pay-Per-Click (PPC) advertising, or email marketing).

Additionally, in a 2019 study conducted by BrightEdge (a marketing technology company), they analyzed the website traffic from several thousand business owners. They found that organic traffic, or SEO, accounted for 53.3% of the total website traffic. Compared to paid search (PPC) and social media - each accounting for 15% and 4.7% of traffic, respectively (BrightEdge, 2019).

So with SEO being so widely used by businesses and industry professionals, you may be wondering, "How is SEO so effective at generating quality traffic to a website?"

Why is SEO Effective

There are many reasons SEO tends to be more effective than other digital marketing channels - indeed, there are too many for us to cover in this book. So let's explore the most common reasons SEO is so effective.

First, search engine users tend to be more engaged and actively focused on finding products and services than social media users, who may be there for entertainment purposes (Crestodina, n.d.).

Another reason for SEO's effectiveness is that search engines have naturally become a prominent place for people to find information in general.

In 2005, Pew Research Center conducted a study, and the results found that 84% of adult internet users in the United States have used search engines to help them find information online (Pew Research Center, 2005).

Additionally, 44% of users reported saying that most or all the information they search for online is *critical* or essential and that they find it to complete their tasks or answer their questions (Pew Research Center, 2005).

With search engines being a staple of everyday life, it makes sense why many business owners and marketers have already taken advantage of this growing market to promote their products and services.

Last Thoughts about What is SEO

SEO is considered to be a crucial part of a solid online marketing strategy as it is arguably one of the most cost-effective forms of marketing on the Internet. With so many people using search engines to find information, it may be wise to implement a sound SEO strategy sooner than later.

There is a lot of competition on the web for the top spots in the search engine results pages. Staying ahead of the competition is imperative, and having an above-average understanding of search engines and how they can help you remain competitive online is vital to SEO success.

In the next chapter, we will explore the history of search engines and how they have become powerful tools for finding information on the web.

Chapter 2: What are Search Engines

Search Engines are computer programs that allow users to search for information on the Internet. They are essentially a network of computers that use **Spiders**, also known as **Web-Crawlers** or **Bots,** to scour the Internet looking for webpages to add to their **Index.**

Users are then able to access the search engine's index through a user interface; this is usually a page that allows the user to enter **queries** or specific questions into a **search bar** to find webpages that meet their needs.

Here is an example of what a search engine user interface may look like:

Once a query has been entered into the search bar, a search is initiated, and the search engine then displays **Hyperlinks** or access points to the content that addresses the query.

The search engine displays the content in a listed fashion on what is called the **Search Engine Results Pages**, also commonly referred to in the SEO field as the **SERPs** (Wall, 2017).

Below is an example of what a search engine results page (SERP) may look like:

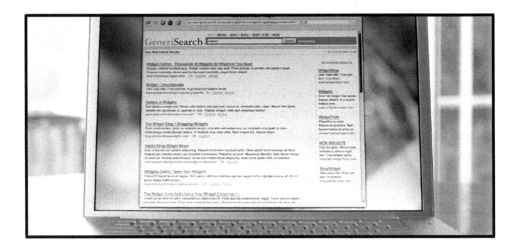

As you can see in the image there is a webpage that includes a "list" of other webpages that a user can visit.

Now that you have a basic idea of what search engines are, let's explore how they came to be.

History of Search Engines

During the early days of the Internet, there wasn't a robust way for people to find documents yet. Internet users often relied on methods like **File Transfer Protocol (FTP)** to download documents and share with others; however, this method was inefficient and often led to a poor user experience.

The first web directory, **Archie**, was created in 1990 by Alan Emtage, a student at Mcgill University in Canada, to help solve the problems created by FTP. Emtage created an "index" or database where users could search for FTP files and share them with others (Wall, 2017).

Archie was revolutionary, but it pales in comparison to modern-day search engines.

According to Slawski (2006):

> Well, it didn't have the capabilities of today's search engines, but
> it did allow you to look around the internet if you knew the name
> of a file you might be looking for. However, Archie didn't index
> the content of text files. That capability came in 1991 with the
> development of another search, known as Gopher. (para. 8)

As a result of Archie's popularity, Emtage teamed up with fellow programmers Farhad Anklesaria, Paul Lindner, Daniel Torrey, and Bob Alberti to develop Archie's successor, **Gopher,** in 1991.

Gopher was a web directory named in honor of the University of Minnesota's microcomputer support department (Edwards, 2021). It exploded in popularity as it was deemed a breakthrough in web directory technology because it allowed users to search for files without requiring any data input.

"Gopher was a real breakthrough. You could search across Gopherspace or just browse a Gopher system through a series of menus and see where it led." (Edwards, 2021)

Gopher eventually became the primary method for searching the Internet by universities and government agencies, who were the primary users of the internet at the time.

Unfortunately, this was short-lived. In 1993, the **World Wide Web** was created by Tim Berners-Lee and presented a more robust web directory.

As the World Wide Web began to take off, Gopher quickly fell out of favor as the Internet became more mainstream and for-profit.

Compared to Gopher, which only used text, the World Wide Web was much more interactive and did not need menus.

It also made navigating the Internet more accessible by introducing **Hyperlinks**, or **Uniform Resource Locators (URLs),** to help users find what they were looking for easier.

According to Edward (2021):

Unlike Gopher, which mostly collected and organized resources,

the WWW was a publishing platform. With graphics now in the

mix, the WWW could easily be adapted for commercial use. (para

23)

Although the World Wide Web was more widely used, it still was not up to the standard of modern-day search engines.

It was simply a directory; there was yet to be a way to gather all the resources and information on the World Wide Web and make them even more searchable.

This is where search crawlers come in.

Web Crawlers Begin Showing Up

In June 1993, Matthew Gray introduced the **World Wide Web Wanderer,** which worked by capturing URLs and storing them in a database, called the **Wandex** (Wall, 2017).

Other crawlers began to pop up as well:

- October 1993: Martijn Koster created **ALIWEB** (Wall, 2017).
- December 1993: Jonathon Fletcher created **Jumpstation** (Wikipedia, n.d.).

- March 1994: Oliver McBryan created the **World Wide Web Worm** (Wikipedia, n.d.).

All the crawlers worked similarly: the crawler would go to a document, analyze its headings and titles, and then store the information in a database. However, this was still relatively primitive as the crawlers had no way to decide which documents should be included in the index and which ones should not.

Things began to shift in the summer of 1994 when crawlers became more advanced.

On July 20th, 1994, **Lycos** went public with a catalog of 54,000 documents. In addition to providing ranked relevance retrieval, Lycos provided prefix matching and word proximity bonuses (Wall, 2017).

Then **Alta Vista** came in December 1995, according to Wall (2017):

> They had nearly unlimited bandwidth (for that time), they were the
>
> first to allow natural language queries, advanced searching
>
> techniques and they allowed users to add or delete their own URL
>
> within 24 hours. (para. 68)

Search crawlers had one more major boost before the new millennium with **Ask Jeeves** in April of 1997, which used human editors to match search queries (Wall, 2017).

Nevertheless, things started to pick up steam at the beginning of the 21st century. Let the search engine wars begin.

Search Engine Wars Begin

By the late 1990s into the early 2000s, things were heating up. Crawlers had accelerated in capabilities and were now becoming fully-fledged *search engines,* or robust databases, used to find information online.

Google was founded in 1998 by Stanford University students Larry Page and Sergey Brin and quickly gained popularity (Wall, 2017). However, it was still far from the titan it is today.

Yahoo! by Jerry Yang and David Filo was founded in 1994. Initially, it was only a web directory (Wikipedia, n.d.). Furthermore, in 2000, Google was chosen as Yahoo!'s search engine provider (Hall, 2022). However, this was short-lived, as Yahoo! dispensed Google in 2004 in an attempt to become their competitor. Yahoo! started utilizing its own proprietary search engine software.

Microsoft Network (MSN)*, created by* **Microsoft** in 1995, was also a key player in the search engine wars (Wikipedia, n.d.).

The battle between these three major search engines continued into the early to late 2000s, with each company trying to gain an edge. However, who took home the search engine war trophy?

Google is the Winner

Google began to take off in 2004 with the help of its webpage ranking software, **PageRank**. Their PageRank software graded the value and relevancy of a webpage based on the number and quality of editorial votes or "backlinks" pointing at it. Then it ranked pages based on the quality of those links (Wall, 2017).

In 2004, it was reported that users were now searching on Google 200 million times a day (Hall, 2022). Thus, Yahoo! and MSN quickly fell out of favor.

Microsoft tried its best to "keep up" with Google by rebranding its search engine MSN to **Bing** in 2009. However, Google remains the most used search engine today, with Google currently holding 89.95% of the global search market share, followed by Bing with 8.88%, and Yahoo! in third place with 2.55% (Theuring, 2022).

Last Words about the History of Search Engines

In a nutshell, search engines began as databases housing files for the use of government and higher institutions. Within the last 30 years, search engines have evolved exponentially. As they have become more robust and available for commercial and public use - they have transformed how we search and receive information.

Search engines have made information easily accessible and have made great strives to ensure that the information we receive is reliable and helpful.

Now that we have outlined search engines' remarkable history, let's explore how they work, and the three-step process they use to match relevant web content with users' search queries.

How Search Engines Work

In general, all search engines operate on the same three-step process: **Crawling**, **Indexing**, and **Serving Search Results**. Below is a graphic depicting this three-step process:

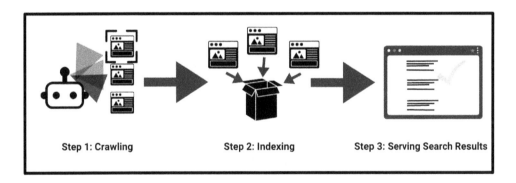

Step 1: Crawling   Step 2: Indexing   Step 3: Serving Search Results

Let's explore what *Crawling* is and how it works.

Step 1: Crawling

Crawling is a process where the Web Crawler looks for new content (webpages, videos, books, PDF files, images, infographics, articles, research papers, etc.) to add to a search engine's index.

Web crawlers are able to find this content through a variety of methods such as:

- user-submitted links to the content
- links on previously visited content to the new content (these are called Internal Links)
- or through a file called an XML Sitemap, which is a file that shows search engines where to find each webpage on a website

We will explore XML Sitemaps and Internal links in more detail in later chapters and sections.

After the crawler accesses a webpage, if it is considered useful then the *indexation* process begins.

Step 2: Indexation

Indexation occurs once a webpage is rendered, crawled, and analyzed by a search engine (Google Search Central, n.d.). Indexing happens through the following process:

- analyzing a webpage's HyperText Markup Language (HTML) elements
- analyzing a webpage's embedded pictures and videos
- analyzing hyperlinks or citations to another website on the crawled page

After conducting the thorough process, the search engine then determines the viability of the web content for the index based on a variety of factors like:

- the content's writing quality
- the website's technical efficiencies
- the originality of the content

In other words, if a webpage is determined to have quality writing, is technically sound, and possesses original content - then the page is likely to be indexed. Moreover, if the webpage does not pass the "tests," it will not be indexed until revisions are made.

Many search engines like Google mention that *indexing isn't guaranteed* (Google Search Central, n.d.). This means that just because you created a webpage, there is no guarantee that a search engine will index it.

Other factors that influence whether your content will be indexed or not include:

- its relevance to the user's query, its quality
- its ability/inability to be crawled designated by a Noindex Meta Tag, or a *"Disallow Rule"* outlined in the Robots.txt File (Google Search Central, n.d.)

We will explore the Noindex Meta Tag and Robots.txt files in more detail, in the Technical SEO chapter.

Once your webpage or content makes it through the "indexing wringer", it now can then be served on the search results pages.

Step 3: Serving Search Results

If a search engine decides to index the content, it will then be served in the search results.

Users can then enter "queries," or words and phrases, to access the indexed content. When a user performs a search, the search engine runs its *algorithm*, or relevancy software, to find web content that it believes best matches what the user is looking for.

The crawler then "ranks" or positions links to the web content on the Search Engine Results Page (SERP). You may recall this information from the beginning of the chapter, but to go into greater detail.

Additionally, the crawler generally places links to the content it believes most closely matches the users' query at the top of the page. The user can then "click" on one of the links to access the web content.

Essentially, this is how the process works. However, I would visit the documentation of all the major search engines, Google, Bing, Yahoo!, DuckDuckGo, and others, to ensure that you know the specific features and *ranking factors* each search engine uses to determine where to rank your website.

Reviewing each search engine's ranking factors will help you better adjust your tactics, strategies, and content to ensure your website gets the best results.

Last Thoughts about Search Engines

Search engines have become a key component of our everyday lives. As time goes on, they continue improving their algorithms to provide more accurate and relevant user results.

Because of that, it is important for you to stay up to date on the latest algorithm changes to ensure that you are not caught off guard if and when significant changes happen.

In the next chapter, we will explore **Keywords** and how they can be used to help signal search engines about the topic and purpose of your webpage.

Chapter 3: Keywords

Let us explore a significant component of a strong SEO strategy: **Keywords**. I will explain what keywords are, why they are essential, and how to use them best to achieve maximum SEO success. Let's dive in.

What is a Keyword

A **Keyword** is a word or phrase that someone may "target" or include on a webpage to increase the webpage's chances of being shown to searchers with a relevant search **Query** or question.

Regarding web content creation, keywords define your content's topic or focus (Moz.n.d.).

You may often hear the words *queries* and *keywords* used interchangeably in the SEO field - but they are different. Let me explain:

Imagine that a user wants information on "***How to make bread?***" To find instructions to help them, the user may pull up their preferred search engine and type in a *query,* such as:

- *What ingredients are in bread?*
- *What do I need to make bread?*
- *Can I make bread without yeast?*
- *Is bread easy to make?*

Essentially *queries* are words, phrases, or questions that a searcher uses to find web content in a search engine's index.

Whereas *keywords* refer to the words or phrases you may want to include in your web content if you wish to have it shown for a related query (Larkin, 2022).

So, for instance, if you wanted to create a webpage that satisfies the query "***How to make bread?***" Some possible keywords you could include on your webpage could be:

- *Bread dough recipe*
- *Homemade bread recipe*
- *Best bread recipe*

Including enough of these relevant keywords in your content may make it easier for a web crawler to find your webpage and show it to searchers who may need it.

In a nutshell, **a keyword is what you use to target queries**. But the question remains: Why should you bother to care about keywords? Let us explore why keywords are essential to SEO.

Why are Keywords Important

Keywords should matter to you because you will be responsible for finding them and deciding which ones are the best to target. Selecting the most relevant keywords can, theoretically, help your webpages prosper on the SERPs.

Conversely, targeting the *wrong* keywords can significantly negatively affect your website's SEO performance because there will be no chance that your webpages will appear for relevant queries.

With these factors in mind, it is imperative to understand how to choose the right keywords through **Keyword Research** and **Analysis**.

What is Keyword Research and Analysis

The strategies you use to find keywords are known as **Keyword Research**, which is the process of identifying the most relevant keywords for a business or website to target for its content (Leist, 2022).

According to Leist (2022):

Keyword research helps you find which keywords are best to target

and provides valuable insight into the queries that your target audience is actually searching on Google. The insight that you can

get into these actual search terms can help inform content strategy

as well as your larger marketing strategy. (para. 3)

You may also hear this process referred to as **Keyword Analysis**.

I like to distinguish between the two because "research," in my opinion, is just finding the keywords, and "analysis" is in choosing what keywords are the easiest and the most relevant to target.

How to do Keyword Research

There are numerous methods to help you find keywords, but if you are just starting, I recommend using the *auto-suggest* feature of your preferred search engine.

The auto-suggest feature is a tool that shows users recommended keywords that may be related to what they are seeking. For the keyword ***bread recipe***, some recommended keywords may be:

- *Bread recipe for beginners*
- *Bread recipe active dry yeast*
- *Bread recipe for bread machine*
- *Easy bread recipe*

With these keywords, you can then decide which ones to target.

The main thing to remember when starting keyword research is to always start with a **Seed Keyword.** A seed keyword is a starter word or phrase you use to find additional keyword ideas.

So in the last example, our seed keyword was "***bread recipe***," but let us pretend your seed keyword is "***pizza.***"

Here is a list of keyword ideas that may appear in the search engine's *auto-suggest*:

- *Pizza takeout*
- *Fast food pizza*
- *Late night pizzeria*
- *Fast pizza delivery*
- *Pizza to-go*

As I stated, you can come up with these ideas by simply using the auto-suggest; however, if you want to take your research a step further, you can use a *commercial keyword research tool*.

Commercial keyword tools work similarly to the auto-suggest feature by letting you input a few seed keywords. Then the tool will output a list of suggested keywords you could target (Soulo, 2022).

Often the suggested keywords are ones you would have never thought of alone. For instance, if I type in *"pizza delivery"* using a tool, here are some suggested keywords I may likely find:

- *Pizza delivery service*
- *Pizza places that deliver*
- *Best pizza delivery*
- *24-hour pizza*
- *Cheap pizza delivery*

Think of the tool as a miniature search engine but for keyword data.

Additionally, here are some other methods:

- Dictionaries
- Thesauruses
- Customer surveys
- Online forums

I will not expand on these additional techniques; they are relatively straightforward. These methods are best to use if you get stuck thinking of keyword ideas.

Now that you know how to find keywords, let us discuss how to choose "good" ones.

How to Choose Good Keywords

When choosing keywords, generally speaking, you want to pay attention to three main things:

1. **Search Volume**
2. **Competition Score**
3. **Search Intent**

As you dive deeper into the SEO field, you will hear about other, more robust metrics to help you decide what keywords are good.

In my opinion, the basic three listed above are the ones all beginners should know. Now let us explore each of these metrics in more detail.

Search Volume

Search Volume is the number of searches per month a particular keyword gets. The amount of searches is estimated and can be subject to seasonal, regional, and thematic fluctuations (Search Metrics, 2022).

Generally speaking, you want to target keywords with thousands of searches per month because this validates that someone is actually using these keywords to find things, but remember it is just a metric.

There are some instances where you can also use keywords that may have *zero* or a very low number of searches per month because, again, this is just an estimate. As long as the keyword is relevant to your audience, you should consider using it.

Competition Score

Competition Score, *keyword difficulty,* or *SEO difficulty*, is how easy or hard it may be to rank a webpage for a particular keyword.

This metric varies from keyword research tool to tool, but in general, this metric is calculated based on the number of "backlinks" or links from referring websites you would need to be able to rank for this keyword (Soulo, 2022).

Theoretically, a keyword with a *higher* difficulty score could take more backlinks for you to rank for it. In general, you want to target keywords with relatively low competition.

However, there are some instances where targeting a high-competition keyword may be best. Again, always choose the keyword that is most relevant to you.

Search Intent

Search Intent, also known as "user intent," is a metric that does not necessarily have a score attached to it.

Understanding the search intent of a keyword is more about analyzing what type of content the searcher prefers when searching for a particular keyword. Or the "main goal" a user has when typing a query into a search engine (BacklinkO, n.d.).

The simplest way to figure this out is to type a keyword into the search engine search bar and see what type of content or webpages comes up on the SERP. So, again back to our *pizza* example.

If you type in "*pizza*," you will likely see pizza restaurants as the top-ranking search results.

This means that search engines discovered that when people type in "*pizza*," they are most likely looking to visit a "*pizza restaurant.*"

However, in comparison, if you type in "*pizza sauce*," the top-ranking pages are recipes for *how to make pizza sauce*.

So, again, this means that search engines determined that when someone types in *pizza sauce*, they are most likely looking for information on how to make it. Now, this is honestly one of the most important metrics when choosing keywords, and here is why:

- To have a website "rank" or show up on the first page of search results for its targeted keywords, you <u>must</u> match search intent.

- Sometimes you may choose a keyword you think is great, but after checking the search intent, you may realize that you do not have the resources or ability to produce content to match the intent.

For example, if you want to rank for the keyword "*pizza*," but you are a food blog, you are better off trying to rank for "*how to make pizza*."

The search intent of "*pizza*" is typically users looking for pizza restaurants, whereas the search intent of "*how to make pizza*" is users looking for pizza recipes - a food blog will likely have that type of content. Therefore, a food blog could easily rank for the keyword "*how to make pizza.*"

According to Webfx (n.d.):

> Previously, optimizing for the keyword was the main focus.
>
> Companies focused on integrating the keywords into their
>
> campaign without regards for the quality of information on the
>
> page. It was about integrating keywords, rather than focusing on
>
> the information attached to those keywords.

Now, Google has gotten smarter, shifting its focus onto the user's experience and providing search results that give searchers the best possible results. It's not enough to just integrate keywords into your campaign. You must now have valuable information that matches and expands on those keywords. Your content and landing pages must be geared towards your audience and their search intent. (paras. 3 - 5)

I would not take this metric lightly because search engines are constantly reworking their algorithms to display the most relevant results.

As time passes, it may become harder and harder to "rank" or show up high on the results pages unless you can accurately match intent. Keep that in mind as you pick keywords.

Let's explore the types of keywords you can choose to target and their purpose.

Types of Keywords

While there are metrics for selecting keywords, there are also different "types" or classifications of keywords.

In the following few sections, let's explore three common types: **Geotags, Short-Tail keywords,** and **Long-Tail keywords**.

Geotags

Geotags are keywords that include the physical location (e.g., city, state, etc.) that a website is in (Si, 2022).

The tags are normally placed in a webpage's *Title Tag*, *Meta Description*, *Image Alt Text*, and in the content itself.

We will explore Title Tags, Meta Descriptions, and more in greater detail in the On-Page SEO chapter of the book.

One reason someone would use geotags is to help a website rank higher when users are searching locally.

Here is an example of some geotags for a dentist in Seattle, Washington:

- *Tooth Repair Seattle*
- *Periodontics Seattle*
- *Dental Crowns Seattle*
- *Cavity Fillings Seattle*
- *Cosmetic Dentistry Seattle*
- *Dentist Seattle*

Do you see how the location of Seattle is in all the keywords? Theoretically, when a Seattle, WA user types in *"Dentist near me"*, a dentist's office with the geotags above on their websites would most likely appear on the first page.

Short-Tail and Long-Tail Keywords

A **Short-Tail Keyword**, or **Broad Keyword,** is a word or phrase that searchers use to find general information, products, or services.

So, if you are a dentist, for example - you are going to want to have the geotags, but you are also going to want to include broad keywords on your site, such as:

- *Dentist*
- *Dental Care*
- *Dental Office*

Searchers may use a broad keyword, like the ones above, if they are unsure of what they need. When searchers are sure of what they need or are looking for, they typically use Long-tail keywords.

A **Long-Tail Keyword** is generally a phrase, question, or string of keywords that a searcher uses to find a "specific" piece of information, product, or service. These keywords are typically longer than broad keywords and have a low number of monthly searches, but this is not *always* the case (Lyons, 2022).

Businesses prefer using long-tail keywords because they are generally easier to rank for and get traffic.

According to Yoast (2021):

> The longer (and more specific) your search terms are, the easier it
>
> is to rank for the term. Because of the vastness of the internet, it is
>
> easier to find your audience for your particular niche. Focusing on
>
> a group of long-tail keywords can result in a great deal of traffic
>
> altogether. (para. 10)

Going back to the Seattle dentist example, some long-tail keywords that they may wish to target are:

- *Teeth cleaning appointment*
- *Same-day tooth cleaning*
- *Prosthetic dentist surgery*

These are precise keywords, and chances are the people using these keywords know exactly what they want.

Ideally, when choosing keywords to target, it may be wise to mix "short" and long-tail keywords. Using a combination of the two will ensure that you are targeting searchers at every stage of their search journey.

Last Words about Keywords

There is undoubtedly more to keywords than what I have explained thus far. The information I have provided will help you gain a foundational understanding of keywords and their purpose in SEO.

Generally speaking, you should choose relevant keywords that have an intent you can match and initiate actions to be taken on your website.

Now that we discussed the basics of keywords, let us get into the three domains of SEO (**Technical**, **On-Page**, and **Off-Page**).

Chapter 4: Technical SEO

Considered the foundation of a strong SEO campaign, **Technical SEO** is the domain of SEO focused on creating and optimizing a website so that search engines can readily crawl, index, and render its content (Indig, 2022).

These modifications allow search engines to efficiently:

- **Crawl**: Find essential webpages, visit them, and determine what they are about
- **Index**: Store the webpages for the future
- **Render**: Show the webpages to users

By having a website that is fast, reliable, and easy to navigate, web crawlers can visit more directories on a website, crawl more webpages, and thus index more content.

This is critical as search engines generally "budget" or cap the time they allot to each website for crawling and indexing. (Google search central, n.d.).

What does this mean?

If a website is difficult to crawl, there is very little chance of having SEO success, as the website's content would never reach the index in the first place and thus would never be seen by searchers.

In this chapter, we are going to explore several key technical components that can be improved or included on a website:

- Web Hosting
- URLs
- Server Response Codes
- Robots.txt File
- XML Sitemap File

- Noindex Meta Tag
- Canonical Tag
- Hreflang Tag
- Core Web Vitals
- Schema Markup

By attending to these technical components, you can ensure that crawlers can make the best use of their limited crawling resources, thus increasing your chances of achieving maximum SEO success.

Before I dive into the elements of technical SEO that can be improved, it is important also to mention one factor that is often beyond a webmaster's control: **Web hosting.**

Web Hosting

For a website to be accessible on the Internet and thus accessible to search engines, the website must be "housed" or stored on a **Server.** A server can also be thought of as a digital neighborhood.

Many web admins may choose to *house* their websites on their own servers. However, generally, hosting is outsourced to a "web hosting service" or companies that have a network/collection of servers that they then "rent" out for other people to house their website (Wikipedia n.d).

Although this may seem like a good idea, using shared hosting can lead to slow website performance and delayed usability.

This can happen due to a variety of factors, such as competition with other websites for server space, the size of the server, how fast the server can process requests, the amount of data that can be transferred at one time, and the amount of traffic the website receives (Donahole, 2020).

In my experience, the only way to mitigate hosting issues is often to upgrade (pay for) a better package or to have a dedicated server, which requires an investment. Both methods are typically expensive for a small business; therefore, drastically improving performance is not always feasible.

Again, it is important for you to know this before you partake in learning the rest of the technical SEO elements because I, for one, have made the mistake of optimizing a website without realizing that there were limitations to how far I could go performance-wise.

Last Words about Web Hosting

Generally, you should choose web hosting that fits your needs, but sometimes the hosting that is required is outside of the budget you have set aside for it.

Understanding the role that hosting plays in the overall technical SEO strategy can help you better prioritize actions that will lead to better performance - rather than spinning your wheels trying to fix something that may be outside the scope of your immediate needs or control.

Now that we discussed web hosting let us talk about the next most important thing: your website and webpage's location on the Internet better known as a **URL**.

URLs

A **Uniform Resource Locator (URL)**, also called a "web address," is the location of a website or file on the Internet. It was developed in 1994 by Tim Berners-Lee as a way to make the World Wide Web easier to use and more accessible (Wikipedia, 2022).

As I mentioned in the *History of Search Engines* section, sharing files in the '90s was a cumbersome process. However, by making the address of a file easy to remember, Berners-Lee made the process of sharing webpages much more accessible.

Here's an example of a basic URL:

`https://www.domain.com/folder/web-page`

Before we dive into URL structure, I want to preface that URLs can be rather *tricky* to comprehend because they can include many components that can be abstract.

Nevertheless, don't worry; in the next section, you can refer to this simple diagram below to clearly understand what I mean.

With that note in mind, let's break down the structure of the URL:

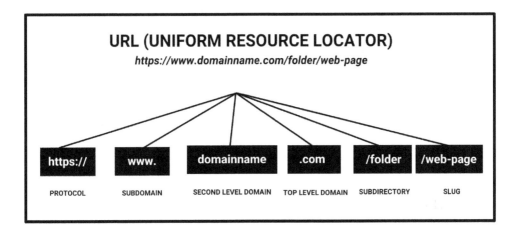

The first piece of a URL is: `https://` this stands for the *Protocol* or the way the website is accessed.

In this case, it is the **HyperText Transfer Protocol Secure (HTTPS)** which is considered to be the most secure way of transferring information on the Internet, as opposed to `http://` which is just **HyperText Transfer Protocol (HTTP)**, which is often avoided because of its less secure nature (Moz n.d.).

Next, `WWW` stands for the World Wide Web. This statement is used to be able to access other webpages in the online directory (Wikipedia, 2022).

WWW is also an example of a **Subdomain** - which can be thought of as a "subdivision" of a *domain* where additional webpages and content can be stored.

domainname is the name of the website (Moz n.d.). It can also be referred to as the **Second level domain (SLD)** or just simply the *domain*.

The .com indicates the type of **Top Level Domain (TLD)**, used in the **Domain Naming System (DNS)**. In this case, it is **commercial** .com but other common TLDs are .edu for education or .org for organizations (Moz n.d.).

/folder indicates the current **Subdirectory** or holding place of the webpage, and lastly, /web-page/ is the name of the webpage, it can also be referred to as a **Slug**.

Why Does URL Structure Matter in SEO

Google mentions that having URLs that include "simple" and "descriptive" words can make it easier for users to understand the focus of the webpage (Google Search Central n.d.).

However, many SEO practitioners also believe that there is a "ranking" benefit from including descriptive terms in a URL.

According to Moz (n.d.):

> URLs are a minor ranking factor search engines use when
> determining a particular page or resource's relevance to a search
> query. While they do give weight to the authority of the overall
> domain itself, keyword use in a URL can also act as a ranking
> factor.

While using a URL that includes keywords can improve your site's search visibility, URLs themselves generally do not have a major impact on a page's ability to rank. (paras. 10 -11)

Essentially, Moz is saying that by including keywords in a URL, there *may* be some benefit, but again there is no definitive proof from Google's documentation that it does.

Last Words about URL Structure

URLs are the main access point a user has to a website and/or webpage, and many search engines like Google recommend using descriptive and intelligible URLs for humans. Additionally, SEO professionals believe that there is a ranking benefit from attending to this measure.

While I have not found anything in any of the major search engine documentation (Google, Bing, and Yahoo!) that vouches for this claim made by many SEOs, I do think it is still worth attending to if you wish to make your URLs easier to read for website visitors in general.

In the next section, we will explore **Response Codes** or alerts that a server gives when a URL request is made, or if an error occurred during the request.

Server Response Codes

When using a server, many problems may arise from time to time that can affect a website's performance and SEO score. Some common server response codes you will deal with in SEO are:

- **200** (OK)
- **500** (Internal Server Error)
- **503** (Service Unavailable)
- **404** (Not Found)
- **301** (Moved Permanently)

- **307** (Temporary Redirect)

A **200** response means that the server is able to find the URL and send it to the users. Basically, everything is working fine.

   500 and **503** are generally out of your control, as this indicates that the *"server is unavailable"* (Avira, n.d.).

In my experience, this happens when the web hosting company is having technical issues.

404 Not Found

Regarding **404 (Not found)**, these errors are typically within your control. This error indicates that a URL link is *broken (*the content does not exist) or the server cannot return the content found at the URL.

From my experience, 404s can arise for one of three reasons:

1. The URL of the link was not entered correctly
2. The webpage was "unpublished" or may not exist yet
3. The webpage was deleted

Here are some potential solutions:

- If it is reason 1, then resolving the error is as simple as entering the correct URL.
- If it is reason 2, you can resolve the issue by publishing the page on the website or creating one.
- And lastly, for reason 3, to resolve the error you will need to redirect the old URL to a new URL and to do this you would implement a *301 (Redirect)*.

301 Redirects

The name **301 Redirect** comes from the response that the server gives when a user accesses the URL but the web content has been "moved permanently" (Payne, 2021).

Essentially, this occurs when the webmaster implements a redirect to a new URL, this is often done via a "plugin" or tool.

In addition to 301 redirects, there are also **307 Redirects** which are temporary redirects. SEOs typically recommend avoiding the use of 307 redirects for security reasons; however, it is still an option available to webmasters.

Last Words about Server Response Codes

In my opinion, it is vital to understand server response codes to help you quickly diagnose technical problems that may arise and be able to fix them.

It is also crucial to understand the meaning of these codes, especially 500, 503, and 404s, because having blocked or broken pages can lead to a poor user experience - which, over time, may result in poor search engine rankings.

In the next section, we will explore two files generally stored on a website that can help search crawlers with crawling and indexing a website: the **Robots.txt File** and the **XML Sitemap**.

Robots.txt File

Pioneered by ALIWEB creator, Martijn Koster in 1994, the *Robots Exclusion Protocol,* now simply known as the **Robots.txt file**, is a file generally stored on a website at the URL slug: `/robots.txt`

It was invented as a way to tell search engine web crawlers which directories or web folders on the website the crawler can access. The file can also be used to specify which folders the crawlers are "blocked" from or *should not/cannot* access on a website (Wall, 2017).

In a nutshell, the robots.txt file contains "directives" "rules" and "references" - which can be thought of as a request to search crawlers regarding the directories you wish to be visited or ignored.

I must emphasize, it is only a **request**, and there is no guarantee the search crawler will "obey" it.

Here is what Google Search Central (2022) has to say on the matter:

> The instructions in robots.txt files cannot enforce crawler behavior to your site; it's up to the crawler to obey them. While Googlebot and other respectable web crawlers obey the instructions in a robots.txt file, other crawlers might not (para. 8).

Based on the quote above from Google, crawlers will follow the request most of the time; however, I want to pose a caveat because the way they process the request and utilize them when choosing how and what content to index, does vary.

It is much easier to explain this in context, so let me first introduce to you, a basic robots.txt file.

Here's how a basic file is formatted:

```
User-agent: *
Disallow: /author/
Allow: /author/archives/

Sitemap: https://bouncerank.com/sitemap_index.xml
```

The file is broken up into three main components:

- User-Agent
- Disallow/Allow Rule
- Sitemap Reference

User-Agent

The **User-Agent** specifies what search crawlers are able to visit a website. A "star" or `*` next to the user-agent indicates that <u>all</u> search crawlers are allowed to visit the website.

Here's what it may look like:

```
User-agent: *
```

But if you want to specify a specific search crawler, then you would add another user-agent line and include the *code* of the crawler you wish to add.

Here are some common crawlers codes (Eaton, 2022):

```
Google - Googlebot
```

```
Bing - Bingbot
```

```
Yahoo! - Slurp
```

```
DuckDuckGo - DuckDuckBot
```

To include a specific crawler in the file, it may look like this:

```
User-agent: Bingbot
```

Generally speaking, specific crawlers are only specified if the webmaster wishes to limit access to a website for a particular crawler.

To explain how to block a specific crawler, I must first explain the *Disallow* and *Allow Rules* and how they are used in conjunction with the user-agent line to block a specific web crawler.

Disallow and Allow Rules

The **Disallow Rule** tells crawlers which web folder/subdirectories it should not visit or are "blocked from". It can also be used to specify which crawlers should not visit the website at all, as I mentioned earlier.

You may also see an **Allow Rule**; this is the opposite of a *disallow rule*, as it tells the search crawlers what subdirectory they can visit that is *inside* of another subdirectory (Content King, 2022).

Essentially with the *allow rule*, a webmaster can allow crawlers to visit a specific secondary directory, even though the top-level directory may be blocked by the *disallow rule.*

To recall the screenshot again:

```
User-agent: *
Disallow: /author/
Allow: /author/archives/

Sitemap: https://bouncerank.com/sitemap_index.xml
```

As you can see, I specified in the `Disallow:` rule that I want to block crawlers from visiting the `/author/` top level directory on my website, but with the `Allow:` rule I specified that crawlers are able to visit the `/archives/` second level directory, that is inside the `/author/` directory.

It is not uncommon to see a robots.txt file that contains a *disallow rule*, but not an allow rule. The reason is, generally speaking, the *allow rule* is *implied.*

What I mean by that is, if a `Disallow:` rule is specified, without an `Allow:` rule, it is essentially being communicated to the web crawler that the whole directory is blocked from crawling.

Unless the webmaster wants to specify a specific directory in the blocked directory to be crawled, then the rule is often left out.

As you can see in the screenshot below, I included only a *disallow rule*, and I specified that I want the /author/ directory blocked from crawling.

```
User-agent: *
Disallow: /author/

Sitemap: https://bouncerank.com/sitemap_index.xml
```

Additionally, with the rules, you are able to specify multiple directories that you want to block or allow to be crawled. For instance, If I want to *disallow* multiple folders, I would simply add another *disallow rule:*

```
Disallow: /admin/
Disallow: /about/
```

As you can see in the code snippet example, I wanted to also block my /admin/ and /about/ directories. Again the same thing can be done for the *allow rule*, if I wanted to allow a *lower-level directory* to be crawled in each of these directories, my file would look like this:

```
Allow: /admin/plugins/
Allow: /about/bio-pages/
Disallow: /admin/
Disallow: /about/
```

One last thing that I want to point out, it is very important to include the "double slashes" or // between the directories names that you are blocking or allowing to be crawled.

As shown below:

```
/directory-name/
```

The double slashes make it clear to crawlers that a "folder" or directory is being specified in the rule. Essentially, without the double slashes, the rule would be invalid.

Now let's discuss how to *block* search crawlers.

Blocking Search Crawlers

As I mentioned earlier, in addition to blocking a specific directory, a specific crawler can be blocked from crawling the website entirely. To achieve this, a webmaster can include a `User-agent:` directive with the crawler code they wish to block and then include a `Disallow:` rule with a single slash `/`

The single slash `/` indicates that the search crawler is barred from visiting <u>all</u> directories; essentially the whole website. It looks like this:

```
User-agent: Bingbot
Disallow: /
```

Additionally, all crawlers can be blocked by including a `User-agent:` directive with a star `*` and a `Disallow:` rule with a single slash `/`

```
User-Agent: *
Disallow: /
```

Generally speaking, you want to avoid having this configuration in your robots.txt file, but there may be instances where you wish to block crawlers entirely.

For instance, if you are performing a website migration and you do not want crawlers visiting the new website until it's done, then you may want to include this specific configuration in the file.

Now let's get into the last component of the robots.txt file, which is the *Sitemap Reference.*

Sitemap Reference

The **Sitemap Reference** tells crawlers the URL, or page path, to get to the sitemap.

In the next section, I will explain in detail what a *sitemap* is and why a website may benefit from one, but for now, just know that it is essentially a "map" search crawlers use to find webpages on a website.

As you can see in the screenshot below, to include the sitemap reference you can simply type the URL of the sitemap:

```
User-agent: *
Disallow: /author/
Allow: /author/archives/

Sitemap: https://bouncerank.com/sitemap_index.xml
```

For my website Bounce Rank, the line would look like this:

```
Sitemap: https://bouncerank.com/sitemap_index.xml
```

And that is the last component you need to include in the file.

Last Words about Robots.txt File

Despite the intricacies of the Robots.txt file, it is not necessarily *required* to be included on a website. However, it is generally best practice to include one.

The reason is the file gives webmasters the opportunity to tell search engines what folders they should crawl. By being able to control what is indexed and crawled, search crawlers can better prioritize indexing content that matters to users and avoid wasting crawl resources on content that is not relevant.

With that in mind, let's discuss the next technical SEO component: The **XML Sitemap**.

XML Sitemap

Another file stored on a website that tells search engine crawlers about the organization of a website's pages is known as the **XML Sitemap**. It is generally stored on a website at the URL slug: `/sitemap.xml`

The file is essentially a "map" that shows web crawlers how to access each *URL* or location of content on the domain; hence the name "sitemap".

Additionally, the file indicates to search crawlers the priority/ hierarchy of pages on the website; and lastly, it can be used to alert search engines about changes to the website.

XML refers to the coding language, *Extensive Markup Language* used to create the file. To give you a bit more context: The use of XML for sitemaps dates back to 2005 when Google launched *The sitemap 0.84 protocol.*

As websites were becoming more and more complex, search engines found it increasingly more difficult to track the numerous changes that website owners were making to their sites (DynoMapper n.d.).

"This led to the creation of XML protocol that made it possible for search engines to effectively track the URLs and boost their search through the placement of all the information in a single page." (DynoMapper n.d.)

Essentially by using XML, search engines are now able to access webpages easier.

Here is an example of a basic XML sitemap configuration:

```
1   <?xml version="1.0" encoding="UTF-8"?>
2   <urlset xmlns="http://www.sitemaps.org/schemas/sitemap/0.9">
3   <url>
4         <loc>https://bouncerank.com/author/rajseo333/</loc>
5   </url>
6   <url>
7         <loc>https://bouncerank.com/what-is-seo/</loc>
8   </url>
9   <url>
10        <loc>https://bouncerank.com/how-to-write-seo-specialist-cover-letter/</loc>
11  </url>
12  </urlset>
```

To help explain in detail the structure of a sitemap, I want to recall Yoast's (2022) article *What is an XML sitemap and why should you have one?* and Woorank's (n.d.) article *What is an XML sitemap?*

Here is how they describe **sitemap structure**:

The first piece is the XML version declaration, which tells search engine crawlers what type of file they are reading:

```
<?xml version="1.0" encoding="UTF-8'?>
```

The next part is the `<urlset>` HTML tag which tells search engines about the protocol, you can see the code snippet below:

```
<urlset
xmlns="http://www.sitemaps.org/schemas/sitemap/0.9"/ >
```

The third part of the sitemap includes the `<url>` HTML tag and the `<loc>` tag *nested* within it. The `<loc>` tag is used to designate the absolute URL or location on the website of the webpage, as shown on the next page.

```
<url>
<loc>https://bouncerank.com/author/rajseo333</loc>
</url>
```

Moving along, the `<url>` tag and the `<loc>` tag configuration can be duplicated to include additional URLs that are located on the website.

Again to recall the screenshot:

```
1   <?xml version="1.0" encoding="UTF-8"?>
2   <urlset xmlns="http://www.sitemaps.org/schemas/sitemap/0.9">
3   <url>
4       <loc>https://bouncerank.com/author/rajseo333/</loc>
5   </url>
6   <url>
7       <loc>https://bouncerank.com/what-is-seo/</loc>
8   </url>
9   <url>
10      <loc>https://bouncerank.com/how-to-write-seo-specialist-cover-letter/</loc>
11  </url>
12  </urlset>
```

As you can see, the URLs listed below are also included in the sitemap, each placed in a `<loc>` tag *nested* in `<url>` tag:

- `https://bouncerank.com/what-is-seo/`
- `https://bouncerank.com/how-to-write-seo-specialist-cover-letter/`

Lastly, there is an additional tag that can be included in the sitemap: the `<lastmod>` tag. This tag is not included in the screenshot; however, the purpose of this tag is to indicate the last time the sitemap was updated.

Here is an example of the `<lastmod>` tag:

```
<lastmod>2022-01-01</lastmod>
```

As I mentioned earlier, this is how a basic XML sitemap is constructed, but the elements/tags that are included can vary depending on the desired outcome and usage by the webmaster.

Last Words about XML Sitemaps

Like Robots.txt files, XML Sitemaps are not required by search engines and do not speed up crawling and/or indexing. Nevertheless, it is good SEO hygiene to include one on a website.

Also, as I mentioned earlier in the *Robots.txt* section, you want to ensure that you include a sitemap reference in your Robots.txt file. This can help make it easier for crawlers to find your sitemap and thus make the best use of it.

In the next section, we will come back to another term that I mentioned earlier in this book, the **Noindex Meta tag**. We will talk about what it is and how it can be helpful.

Noindex Meta Tag

The `noindex` rule, also referred to as a **Noindex Meta Tag** or simply the *No index tag*, is a directive that can be specified in the **Robots Meta tag** (a tag placed in the HTML `<head>` of a webpage).

The rule is used to tell search engines <u>not to index</u> or include a specific URL/webpage in their database (Ahrefs n.d.).

Below is an example of what the code snippet may look like:

```
<meta name="robots" content="noindex">
```

The no index tag is considered to be a *directive* or an almost exact order for search engines to follow. The reason I say almost "exact" is because *most* search engines will follow the directive.

Google, for example, does follow this directive, and here is what their documentation says on the matter:

"When Googlebot crawls that page and extracts the tag or header, Google will drop that page entirely from Google Search results, regardless of whether other sites link to it." (Google Search Central, 2023).

Many SEO professionals, such as myself, recommend using the no index tag instead of disallowing a webpage in the robots.txt file for content you do not want indexed by search engines.

The reason is content that is blocked can still be crawled by search engines and indexed. This can be an issue, as crawling resources would be wasted on a blocked page. So keep that in mind when implementing no index tags.

Last Words about the Noindex Meta Tag

The Noindex Meta Tag is rather straightforward. Essentially, you use it to control what content you want or do not want search engines to index.

The disallow directive in the robots.txt file also can be used to "block" search engines from certain URLs; however, search engines can ignore this directive, crawl, and potentially index your page.

The noindex meta tag is the most effective way to ensure that URLs you do not want to be indexed will be "hidden" from search engines.

In the next section, we are going to explore two more additional tags: **Canonicals** and **Hreflangs**.

Canonical Tag

A **Canonical Tag** `rel="canonical"` is a piece of HTML code that is added to webpages to tell search engines which page is the original or the preferred version of a page to index (Hardwick, 2022).

Generally, the tag is used to mitigate crawling issues that may arise when multiple pages on a website contain the same or similar information; this is often referred to as ***Duplicate content*** (Google Search Central, n.d.).

There are many ways to specify a *canonical*, but the most common way is via the HTML `<head>` element of the webpage deemed to be the duplicate.

In the `<head>` section, this HTML code snippet below is added:

```
<link rel="canonical" href="https://example.com/sample-page"/>
```

The `<link>` element indicates that you are linking to another page; the `rel="canonical"` indicates which page is a duplicate of another page, and then the `href="https://example.com/sample-page/"` indicates the URL of the page you are setting as the original source of content.

Below I included a diagram to help you make sense of this concept:

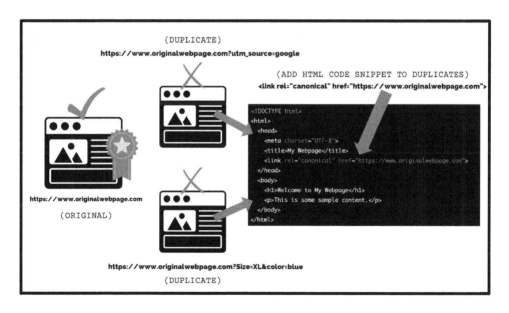

As you can see in the diagram, the original webpage version being designated by the canonical tag is:

```
https://www.originalwebpage.com
```

To indicate to search engines that this is the original source of content, as you can see in the diagram, you add the code snippet (shown below) to each of the duplicate pages' HTML `<head>` element:

```
<link rel="canonical"
href="https://www.originalwebpage.com"/>
```

Last Words about the Canonical Tag

In general, the Canonical Tag is the preferred method to specify to search engines the original source of a piece of content, in instances where there is duplicate content in the index.

While every website owner may not deal with duplicate content, it is important to be aware of the canonical tag and how it can help you with your SEO efforts.

I would also like to add that although a webmaster can add a canonical tag to a webpage, the tag is not considered a *directive* but a *hint* to search engines on which is the canonical or the most relevant page version.

In other words, just because a canonical tag is specified does not mean that the search engines will obey it. Keep that in mind if and when you choose to implement the tag.

Okay, now let's discuss **Hreflang Tags**.

Hreflang Tag

An **Hreflang Tag** is a piece of HTML code that you add to a webpage's `<head>` element to indicate to search engines the languages and countries you are targeting for an alternate version of the webpage.

The snippet is used to help search engines show the correct copy of the page to users in a specific language and country. Here's an example of what the code snippet looks like (Google Search Central, n.d.):

```
<link rel="alternate" hreflang="lang_code"
href="url_of_page" />
```

The `<link>` HTML element indicates that you are linking to another page, the `rel="alternate"` indicates the relationship between the two linked documents and that they are different versions of the same page.

The `hreflang="lang_code"` is where you insert the specific code for the language you wish to target, such as *en* for English, *fr* for French, *es* for Spanish or *de* for German (Pokorny, 2022).

Lastly, the `hreflang="url_of_page"` is the URL of the page you wish to associate with the alternate language. This is the webpage that you want to be shown to users in another language.

On the next page I included a diagram to help you make sense of this concept:

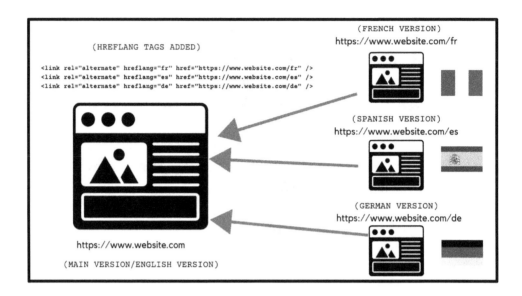

As you can see in the diagram above, the main version, or English version of the page: `https://www.website.com` , has three hreflang tags added to it; one for each alternate language version of the webpage; *French*, *Spanish*, and *German*. As you can see in the code snippets below:

```
<link rel="alternate" hreflang="fr" href="https://www.website.com/fr" />
<link rel="alternate" hreflang="es" href="https://www.website.com/es" />
<link rel="alternate" hreflang="de" href="https://www.website.com/de" />
```

The `hreflang` elements of each tag includes the language codes; *fr* (french), *es* (Spanish) and *de* (German), and then the href attributes include the corresponding copy of the page for that language (e.g. "`https://www.website.com/fr`").

When using hreflang tags, the desired outcome is that search engines will recognize the content as being available in alternate languages.

Therefore, when users are in France, they will see the French version of the page; if they are in Spain, they will see the Spanish; and if the user is in Germany, they will see the German version.

Why Hreflang Tags Matter for SEO

Hreflang tags serve several vital purposes for SEO. First, they indicate the relationship between different language versions of a page, which keeps your website relevant in the eyes of search engines.

De Valk (2022) reports:

> If you have a version of a page that you have optimized for the users' language and location, you want them to land on that page. Because having the correct language and location-dependent information improves their user experience and thus leads to fewer people bouncing back to the search results. And fewer people bouncing back to the search results leads to higher rankings. (para. 6)

Second, they prevent instances of duplicate content.

De Valk (2022) continues:

> If you have the same content in English on different URLs aimed at the UK, the US, and Australia, the difference on these pages might be as small as a change in prices and currency. But without hreflang, Google might not understand what you're trying to do and see it as duplicate content. With hreflang, you make it very clear to the search engine that it's (almost) the same content, just optimized for different people. (para. 7)

Google recommends that you use hreflang tags preemptively, rather than have them decide on which copy of the page to use:

"Note that even without taking action, Google might still find alternate language versions of your page, but it is usually best for you to explicitly indicate your language- or region-specific pages." (Google Search Central, n.d.)

The quote above further emphasizes the benefit of using this tag for SEO.

Last Words about Hreflang Tags

Hreflang Tags are most important for individuals doing *International SEO,* but it is still beneficial to know them and have some understanding of how they work.

Also, based on Google's recommendations, it is essential to use them to have a quality user experience across regions and languages if you have multiple versions of your site.

In the upcoming section, we will explore **Core Web Vitals** and how they are used to assess a website's overall speed and performance.

Core Web Vitals

The **Core Web Vitals** is a report provided by Google that shows the performance of each website's unique webpages or URLs. Based on user data, it assesses a website's overall user experience (UX), speed, and performance.

Typically, when you hear SEOs say *"Core Web Vitals"* they are likely referring to the three metrics that Google measures to compare each URL based on user data (Google Search Central, 2022):

- Cumulative Layout Shift (CLS)
- First Input Delay (FID)
- Largest Contentful Paint (LCP)

However, the report is more comprehensive than the three metrics mentioned above. The core web vitals report consist of the following diagnostics (Google Search Central, 2022):

- Status (Poor, Need improvement, Good)
- Metric type (CLS, FID, LCP)
- URL group (groups of similar webpages)

The purpose of the report is to measure a webpage's overall *User experience (UX)* and performance. In other words, the report assesses how easy it is for a user and search crawler to navigate and access each component of a webpage.

Many SEO professionals believe that improving on CLS, FID, and LCP specifically can lead to more favorable rankings on search engine result pages.

Here are Stox's (2022) thoughts on the matter:

> There are over 200 ranking factors, many of which don't carry
>
> much weight. When talking about Core Web Vitals, Google reps
>
> have referred to these as tiny ranking factors or even tiebreakers.
>
> (para. 14)

As Stox highlights in the statement above, improving core web vitals will not create a significant ranking boost; however, we can *assume* that if two incredibly similar websites are competing for a ranking position - Google will essentially favor the website with better core web vitals.

BacklinkO (n.d.) expands on this topic and reports the following:

> It's important to point out that a great page experience score won't
>
> magically push you to the #1 spot in Google. In fact, Google was

quick to point out that page experience is one of several

(approximately 200) factors that they use to rank sites in search.

(para. 8)

While it may not lead to an alarming ranking boost, it may still be worth improving in order to improve the quality of a website as a whole.

Now let us explore each core web vital metric outlined in the report in greater detail.

Largest Contentful Paint

Largest Contentful Paint (LCP) measures how long it takes the "largest content element" to render and become visible in a user's device viewport from the moment in time when the user first visits the webpage. Google points out that this is often a picture or video (Google Search Central, n.d.).

LCP measures in seconds. A score of *2.5 seconds* or less is the desired score for optimal performance, and anything over *4 seconds* is a possible reason for alarm.

The LCP is arguably the most crucial part of the report, as it is a key factor that Google uses to evaluate a website's "loading time" or speed, and because of that, it may be worth improving it for a sound SEO strategy.

According to Rocket Content (2020):

Over the past few years, Google has increasingly focused on

defining evaluation parameters to enhance the user experience, all

of them integrating Core Web Vitals.

As LCP is related to page loading time, it naturally influences how

Google analyzes and ranks a site on the results page. (para. 21)

Overall LCP is a very significant part of the Core Web Vitals and should not be ignored if you wish to provide a fast and user-friendly experience for your website visitors.

Let's explore the next metric: *First Input Delay (FID)*.

First Input Delay

First Input Delay (FID) is a measure of the time it takes for the browser to respond to the first interaction a user has with the webpage. The interaction can be something like clicking a button, or a link (Google Search Central, n.d.).

According to Google Search Central (n.d.):

This measurement is taken from whatever interactive element that

the user first clicks. This is important on pages where the user

needs to do something, because this is when the page has become

interactive" (para. 13)

FID is measured in milliseconds, with a score of *100 ms* or less showing good performance while a score of over *300 ms* indicating poor performance.

A key point to consider about FID is that it often depends on the web browser or the application the users use to access the Internet. Walton (2019) reports:

As developers who write code that responds to events, we often

assume our code is going to be run immediately—as soon as the event happens. But as users, we've all frequently experienced the

opposite—we've loaded a webpage on our phone, tried to interact

with it, and then been frustrated when nothing happened. In

general, input delay (a.k.a. input latency) happens because the

browser's main thread is busy doing something else, so it can't

(yet) respond to the user. (para. 9)

Walton's statement highlights the importance of utilizing code that is not only interactive for the users but is also responsive to the various actions that the users are taking; this ensures that users can have a smooth experience while ensuring that your website can be accessed efficiently by web crawlers.

Now let's unpack the last Core Web Vitals metric: *Cumulative Layout Shift (CLS)*.

Cumulative Layout Shift

Cumulative Layout Shift (CLS) is the sum of all individual layout shift scores for every unexpected movement of the webpage that occurs while it is in use.

This Core Web Vital metric is evaluated by numbers between *zero* and 1, with a CLS of *0.1* being the target, and a CLS of over *0.25* indicating a need for improvement (Google Search Central, n.d.).

Similar to the LCP, an image or video is often the reason for a poor score.

Walton (2019) states:

> The culprit might be an image or video with unknown dimensions,
>
> a font that renders larger or smaller than its fallback, or a third-
>
> party ad or widget that dynamically resizes itself. (para. 3)

Essentially, CLS measures how much a webpage moves around while a user is interacting with it. If a page is moving around too much, this may indicate that there are elements on the page not properly sized and/or formatted.

Google Search Central (n.d.) provides additional clarification on why the CLS metric is used:

> This is important because having pages elements shift while a user
>
> is trying to interact with it is a bad user experience. If you can't
>
> seem to find the reason for a high value, try interacting with the
>
> page to see how that affects the score. (para. 11)

This quote provides additional insight into why improving this metric may be worth your time.

Time To Interactive and First Contentful Paint

I also want to point out two additional metrics worth considering when assessing a website's performance:

- **Time To Interactive (TTI)** which measures how long it takes the webpage to be fully usable after being requested (Chrome developers, 2019).
- **First Contentful Paint (FCP)** which is a measure of when the browser first renders any image, video or text (MDN Contributors, 2022).

TTI and FCP are important as they both provide additional context for how well a webpage can be rendered and interacted with.

But in general, if you have a firm understanding of the three Core Web Vitals (LCP, FID, CLS) you are more than versed enough to be able to improve a website's speed and performance.

Last Words about Core Web Vitals

I am providing you with the Core Web Vitals information from an objective perspective to help you better understand them. I hope this information will help you decide whether you should improve the core web vitals or *if you can.*

As I mentioned earlier in the chapter, web hosting can often be an unexpected and uncontrollable limitation on your website's ability to achieve optimal speed and performance.

Additionally, I've found that using a thin *Content Management System (CMS)*, can also poorly impact your core web vitals. Inefficient CMS' often have built-in limitations that keep you from achieving a pristine core web vital score.

In the following section, we will explore the last technical SEO component worth attending to for a beginner, which is **Schema Markup**.

Schema Markup

Schema Markup, also known as *Schema.org structured data*, is a library of code that includes *microdata,* referred to as "tags," or identifiers you can add to parts of a website's HTML code to help search engines better read and interpret the context of your content. The library comprises different types of "markups" that Google, Bing, Yandex, and Yahoo! provided in collaboration (Moz, n.d.).

Since search engines are mostly a network of computers, they don't necessarily understand the "intent" or goal of a piece of web content.

Hence, it can be harder for them to deliver the best results to a user searching for a particular piece of information.

According to Google Search Central's YouTube channel (2022):

> The web is a very loosely structured collection of documents…but
>
> we need that data to be more structured to apply visual features…
>
> while we have technology to find that "structure" in webpage text
>
> automatically, those systems are not perfect, that's where you
>
> come in. (Google Search Central, 2022, 1:05)

Schema markup helps search engines understand the intent of your content by highlighting the most important aspects of your webpage and letting them know what type of information it contains.

Let's imagine your content includes a "question" - a search engine may not necessarily understand that it is a *question*, or in other words, it may not understand that the goal of your sentence was to gain information about a topic. The search engine may just interpret it as a *statement*.

For instance:

***Is pizza made in America?* (Question)**

May be interpreted as:

***Is pizza made in America.* (Statement)**

Schema markup can help to curve this "miscommunication" because it allows you to format your question in a way that search engines can understand.

In the image below you can see a code snippet example of *FAQ Schema Markup*:

```
<script type="application/ld+json">
{
  "@context": "https://schema.org",
  "@type": "FAQPage",
  "mainEntity": {
    "@type": "Question",
    "name": "Is Pizza made in America?",
    "acceptedAnswer": {
      "@type": "Answer",
      "text": "Pizza, as we know it today, has its roots in Italy. However, it was brought to the United States by
Italian immigrants in the late 19th and early 20th centuries. Since then, pizza has become a staple of
American cuisine and has evolved to include many different regional styles and toppings. In the United
States, there are many popular pizza chains and independent pizzerias that make their own unique versions
of pizza. Some of the most well-known American pizza styles include New York-style, Chicago-style, and
California-style pizza.So while pizza itself may have originated in Italy, it has certainly been adapted and
popularized in the United States and is now considered a quintessential American food."
    }
}
```

As you can see in the image of FAQ schema, you can add your "question" and you can also add an "answer".

Additionally, using schema markup gives you a chance to get an "enhancement", or a *rich snippet.* This is where the webpage search result is larger and takes up more space on the user's screen.

Schema markup is prized by SEO professionals in particular because it is believed that there is a correlation between getting a *rich snippet* and the increased likelihood of a user clicking on the result by 30% (Bruemmer, 2011).

Although schema markup can lead to correlational SEO improvements, Google clearly highlights that it is not causational, as schema markup is not a ranking factor.

Again to cite Google Search Central's Youtube channel (2019):

> From our point of view, (well) they might have spent more time
>
> doing these things technically correct but does that mean the page
>
> is actually a better search result, is that really something that

provides more value to the user or is it just that someone was a little bit smarter in creating that page and the actual content people would read is not actually that much better.

So that's…kind of the tricky balance there and I don't see that changing in the sense that we would suddenly say any page with structured data will have a ranking boost because structured data is invisible so even that would be something that we would be ranking things higher for technical reasons that users would not even be able to appreciate. (Google Search Central, 2019, 32:28)

Although Google clarifies that schema markup doesn't have a direct impact on ranking, it's benefits should not be underestimated.

I have composed a table including all the different types of schema markup. I included the list in a table format to help you better understand each of the schema types and possible usage for designated parts or types of web content.

Different Types of Schema Markup (Xu, 2018):

Schema Markup Type	Potential Uses
Organizational Schema	Generally for companies, or large established brands
Person Schema	Generally to highlight a specific important figure or person
Local Business Schema	Generally for businesses that have physical locations locally

Product Schema	Generally for eCommerce websites
Breadcrumbs	Used to help users know what webpage they are on
Article Schema	Generally meant for highlighting news articles or editorials
How-To Schema	Generally for highlighting how-to guides or step-by-step instructions
Video Schema	Generally to highlight video content on a webpage
Recipe Schema	For highlighting recipe content or how-to guides for foods
Event Schema	For highlighting events, shows, festivals or concerts

This list is not exhaustive. You can visit Schema.org for a complete list of all schema markup types.

Last Words about Schema Markup

Despite not being a ranking factor, Schema Markup is still a great tool to have in your arsenal to increase the *potential* of someone clicking on your website when they see it on search engines.

When getting started with schema markup, I would recommend trying out one markup type at a time to see how it affects your website.

Additionally, in my experience, when you mix too many schema markup types at once, you run the risk of search engines ignoring the markup completely. So keep that in mind when testing out different schema markup types.

Final Words about Technical SEO

Congratulations on completing the Technical SEO chapter of the book! Honestly, this was the **hardest** part of the book to write and edit because I wanted to ensure that I included detailed and thorough information on technical SEO.

Most SEO professionals would agree that technical SEO is the hardest to learn as a beginner. It requires a high level of problem-solving and abstract thinking.

You may discover, as you practice technical SEO, that all the components we discussed are not applicable *all the time*, and if they are, they are only a *momentary* focus of your overall SEO strategy.

In a nutshell, technical SEO is more about *maintenance* rather than consistent development like the other two domains of SEO are. So keep that in mind as you continue on your SEO journey.

Before wrapping up my last thoughts, I would like to offer a piece of advice on how you can practice and hone your technical SEO skills: get a website, or if you are savvy enough, make one from scratch.

When I was learning technical SEO, I made the decision to create a website from start to finish, and it was very rewarding because it taught me about a website from a granular perspective. Which, in my opinion, I believe can go miles in helping you make sense of these abstract concepts.

To aid with this, in the next chapter, we are going to explore the basics of **HyperText Markup Language (HTML)**. The HTML chapter will help familiarize you with the coding language most relevant to SEO.

I will breakdown how it is used to create and structure content on the web. You can use this information to help you with creating a website. Let's jump in!

Chapter 5: HyperText Markup Language (HTML)

HyperText Markup Language (**HTML**) is the *standard markup* or computer code used to create and structure content on the web. Web browsers can *render* (display) HTML on a user's computer screen in a format readable by the user (Wikipedia, n.d.).

Another invention of World Wide Web creator Sir Timothy John Berners-Lee, HTML was designed, in 1989, as an easy-to-use and effective method for creating documents for the Web.

At the time, the Internet was still in its infancy, and there wasn't a straightforward way to create and structure content on webpages.

As I mentioned in the *History of Search Engines* chapter, users often would send FTP (File Transfer Protocol) files to each other to display their work online. Still, these files were often bulky, fragmented, and not easily searchable or accessible to other users.

HTML addressed this issue by allowing developers to embed their content in the form of clickable text, or *Hypertext,* which users can create using *Elements*, also referred to as *Tags*. Tags are specific pieces of code meant to represent the parts of the document.

The tags are similar to the common features of a book (e.g., titles, headers, paragraphs, lists, etc.).

To make things even more accessible, users can "link" or connect documents using *Hyperlinks.* Over time HTML has evolved to include other elements, but the same basic functionality remains today (Wikipedia, n.d.).

On the next page, is an example of a basic HTML document (W3School, n.d.):

```
<!DOCTYPE html>
<html>
    <head></head>
        <body>
        <h1>This is a heading</h1>
        <p>This is a paragraph.</p>
        </body>
</html>
```

As you can see, HTML documents include several key features, such as: `<!DOCTYPE html>` ; this statement declares that the document is an HTML document. All HTML documents must include this statement.

Next is the `<html>` element, which defines the start of the HTML document, followed by a `<head>` element.

You may recall the `<head>` element from the *Canonical Tag* and the *Hreflang Tag* sections of the *Technical SEO* chapter. As I mentioned previously, the tag represents the top or beginning of the HTML document.

In the next section, let's explore the properties and unique syntax of HTML.

Properties and Syntax

Generally, all HTML tags end with a **Closing tag**. For example, referring back to the code snippet on the last page, you can see that the `<html>` element also includes `</html>` as the closing tag.

Most HTML elements include a closing tag. There are a few exceptions, like an `<img>` element, that does not include one.

Another interesting thing about HTML is that you are able to **Nest,** or place other HTML elements inside of each other.

As you can recall from the previous code snippet I showed on the last page:

```
<!DOCTYPE html>
<html>
    <head>
```

Inside of the `<!DOCTYPE html>` element, the `<html>` is nested inside of it, and then nested inside of it, is the `<head>` element.

But there can also be other elements nested inside of the `<head>` element, some of them are required for optimal search engine performance.

According to W3School (n.d.), for Google and other search engines to consider the HTML document valid, typically the `<head>` section must include:

- `<title>` This snippet indicates the title or name of the document.

- `<meta name="description" content=""/>` This is a description of the document, also known as the *meta description.*

- `<meta charset="UTF-8" />` This code snippet indicates the *character encoding* or the types of symbols, and text used in the document. This matters because different languages have different symbols and characters, so using *UTF-8,* which is the standard that most search engines prefer, covers all of the possible characters used in any language.

- `<meta http-equiv="X-UA-Compatible" content="IE=edge" />` This code snippet ensures that all Web browsers (Internet Explorer, Mozilla Firefox, Chrome, etc.) are able to properly display the document.

- `<meta name="viewport" content="width=device-width, initial-scale=1.0" />` This code snippet ensures that the document is viewable on all devices, especially mobile devices.

After the `<head>` section, there is the `<body>` section which represents the content of the document.

Again, referring to the code snippet example from the beginning of the chapter, the `<h1>` tag (First-page header) and `<p>` tag (paragraph text) were nested in the `<body>` section.

```
<body>

<h1>This is a heading</h1>
<p>This is a paragraph.</p>

</body>
```

In the last section of the HTML chapter, we are going to explore some common HTML tags that SEO practitioners, in particular, should be aware of.

Common HTML Tags

Here are some additional common HTML tags you may encounter, (Melnick, 2017):

- `<img src="">` tag which is used to display images and pictures.

- `alt=""` which is an *attribute* or descriptor added to an image to tell search engines and users what the image is.

- `<h2> <h3> <h4> <h5> <h6>` These are smaller, more descriptive headings than the h1, with the section being more in detail as the heading increases.

- `<ul> <ol>` used to represent unordered and ordered list.

- `<a href="URL"> Insert Text Here </a>` This snippet is for an *anchor tag* which is a *hyperlink* and used to link to another HTML document.

- `<div>` used to represent a section, it is also called a *block-level element* because it is displayed on one line, and pushes non-block elements below or to the side of the block element.

Last Words about HTML

The key thing to remember about HTML is that it is a way to construct the different parts of a webpage and make them visually attractive and functional for web browsers. This is the reason why it is so widely used.

It is also the reason why Google, and other search engines define the bulk of their algorithm ranking factors around ensuring that they send users to websites that have well-structured HTML pages.

In the next chapter, we are going to discuss the next domain of SEO, **On-Page SEO**. I hinted at this chapter with the *Common HTML Tags* section in the *HTML* chapter.

You will soon see that these are the same HTML elements you optimize for On-Page SEO.

This is a key chapter for most beginners because this is the part of SEO that explores the *user-facing* elements of a website that users can see and interact with.

By firmly understanding these concepts, you will be able to improve the look and feel of a website to make it easier for users to decipher and find the information they need. Let's dig in!

Chapter 6: On-Page SEO

On-Page SEO, also referred to as *On-Site SEO*, is the domain of SEO that is focused on adding, modifying, or rewriting HTML Elements on a website. These additions or modifications helps search engines to better be able to understand the website's information.

It is believed by SEO practitioners that the better a search engine comprehends a website's content, the more likely they are to "reward" the website by showing its content higher on the SERPs (Moz, n.d.).

Generally, the purpose of on-site SEO is to make the HTML elements on a webpage more useful for humans and search engines. To fulfill this purpose, you need to fill the elements in with information and **keywords,** or phrases, that people are searching for.

In theory, adding keywords to the webpage makes the HTML tags more *semantic* or have more meaning to searchers so that they can easily find the information they are looking for.

Additionally, this is also believed to help search engines understand the content of the page - and *potentially* recommend it to other searchers.

In my opinion, this part of SEO is relatively easier to learn and comprehend than technical SEO, as the concepts are a bit more concrete. I would also like to point out that on-page SEO tends to require more of a creative thinking process rather than a technical approach.

So if you are a creative person or a writer by nature, then on-page SEO is definitely the domain that may grab your attention. But if you are more of a logical thinker, it may be beneficial to work with a copywriter or a content marketer to help you with this domain of SEO.

In this chapter, we are going to explore several on-site SEO elements that you can improve on a website such as:

- Title Tags
- Meta Descriptions
- Image Alt Text
- Headers (H1, H2, H3, H4, H5 and H6)
- Hyperlinks

For each element, I included the HTML code snippet of the element to help you see how each of them are structured and what best practices for each of them are.

Let's dive into on-page SEO, starting with **Title Tags**.

Title Tag

Title Tags, also referred to as *Meta Titles* or *Title Links,* are used by searchers to see what the name of a webpage is and for some insight into what the page is about, thus enticing them to click on it (Moz n.d.).

Think of this tag as the title of a book or a movie. Title tags are helpful to users, but they are also valued by search engines:

"Title links are critical to giving users a quick insight into the content of a result and why it's relevant to their query. It's often the primary piece of information people use to decide which result to click on, so it's important to use high-quality title text on your webpages." (Google Search Central, n.d.)

As an HTML element, a title tag is included in the <head> of a webpage, and it looks like the following:

```
<head><title>Text here</title></head>
```

Text here *is "dummy" text meant to hold the place of a real title. So this is where you would add the title of your webpage.*

On the next page I included an example of what a title tag might look like on search results:

What is Off-Site SEO and Why Does it Matter? - Bounce Rank
Off-Site SEO is about getting backlinks or other websites to link to you. It helps improve your domain authority and rankings.

The top most piece of text: "What is Off-Site SEO and Why Does it Matter? - Bounce Rank" is the title tag. Although the picture does not reflect the color, generally the tag is highlighted with clickable *"purple text."*

Lastly, I want to share that you are not able to see a title tag on the visual front end of a website - to see it, you must view the website's HTML code.

Search engines, on the other hand, are able to easily see the tag and display it to searchers in the SERPs.

Last Words about Title Tags

Generally, the Title Tag is one of the first elements on a webpage that a searcher sees. So because of that, it is important to write tags that are not only descriptive but also enticing enough to want to be clicked on.

There is no concrete evidence that preferential treatment is given by search engines for having an optimized title tag or for having one *at all*. But it may still be worth it to take your time and write title tags that are informative and engaging.

Now let's explore **Meta Descriptions**.

Meta Description

The second text that a searcher sees for each search result is called the **Meta Description**, also known as a *Snippet*. Similar to the Title Tag, the goal of the *meta* is to entice a reader to click on the webpage.

Additionally, search engines use the meta description to explain to searchers what a webpage is about (Google Search Central, n.d.).

Google's documentation mentions that meta descriptions can be influenced in one of two ways:

1. Through the user-specified text in the `<meta>` HTML tag in the `<head>` section for example, like:

```
<head><meta name="description" content="Text here"/></head>
```

2. Or through structured data (i.e., Schema Markup), I already did a thorough breakdown of schema markup in the *Technical SEO* section of the book, so feel free to refer back and read that section for further clarity.

Here is an example of a meta description:

What is Off-Site SEO and Why Does it Matter? - Bounce Rank
Off-Site SEO is about getting backlinks or other websites to link to you. It helps improve your domain authority and rankings.

While the title tag is the uppermost piece of text, the meta description is the lower piece of text placed directly below.

Similar to the title tag, you generally are not able to see the meta tag on the website. Instead, you have to view the website's HTML code to see it. But, again, search engines are able to see the tag and display it to searchers in the SERPs.

Last Words about Meta Descriptions

Similar to the title tag, Meta Descriptions are also an element on a webpage that may influence a searcher's decision to visit the webpage.

Again, like title tags - it is worth your time to write quality meta descriptions for each webpage.

There are instances where search engines may rewrite the meta description you wrote, but it is still helpful to write one anyway to provide additional information about the context of the page.

And, in the event that they do choose to show your description in the search results, it can also provide additional control over what searchers will see and interpret about the page before clicking.

Next, let's explore **Image Alt Text**.

Image Alt Text

Image Alt text is used to describe an image to a user, or search engine crawler. The text is normally invisible to users, but if the image is unable to be loaded, it is then displayed by the browser (Harvard University, n.d.).

It can also appear and be read out loud if a visually impaired user is using a *screen reading device*.

Here's what the text looks like in HTML:

```
<img alt="text here" />
```

And here is an example of what alt text looks like on a browser:

SEO Manager For Hire Raj Clark

In the example, the icon shows that the image could not be "loaded," and next to the icon is the *alt text* that describes what the image is about or represents. In this case, I had a photo of myself, and the alt text was my name and my job title at the time.

Out of all the on-site factors, this one, in my experience, is often the most overlooked. Website owners often just leave the text *empty*, or they have text that does not accurately describe the photo.

Leaving the alt text blank may make it more difficult for users with visual impairments to fully access and experience the webpage. This is an instance where it's important to put SEO aside and instead think about the user and how having meaningful alt text will help them.

Last Words about Image Alt Text

As I mentioned in the section, Image Alt Text is something that is often forgotten or overlooked - but is so crucial for user experience. Alt text provides a great opportunity to make a website more accessible to all users.

I believe filling out your alt text can go leaps and bounds towards making a website more attractive to search engines as well. So again, I think it is worth it to take the extra time, and effort to write alt text that accurately describes the image users are seeing.

Let's move forward and the next on-site SEO element: **Headers**.

Headers (H1, H2, H3, H4, H5, and H6)

Similar to chapters in a book, **Headers,** or *HTML Headings,* can be used to help separate ideas and paragraphs in web content.

Essentially, headers are used to structure content to show readers that the writer is going into more detail about a particular topic.

Additionally, headings matter to search engines because they help them better understand the *hierarchy* of the text on the page, and evaluate its usefulness for searchers (Google search central, n.d.).

On the next page is what headings look like in HTML:

```
<body>
     <h1>text here</h1>
     <h2>text here</h2>
     <h3>text here</h3>
     <h4>text here</h4>
     <h5>text here</h5>
     <h6>text here</h6>
</body>
```

As you can see, I included the `<body>` tag element in the example to show you that heading tags are typically used in the main content of a page.

Below I provided an image of what heading elements can look like on the front-end of a website's design. The first arrow points to the `<h1>` tag, and the second points to the `<h2>` tag.

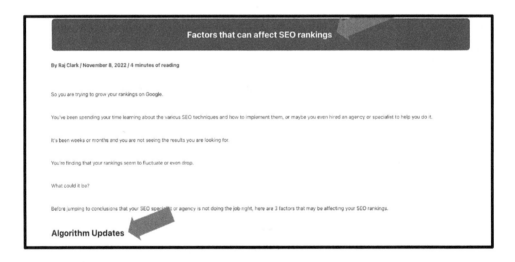

As you can see in the photo, the `<h1>` tag is generally the largest heading, and appears at the top of the webpage.

Whereas the `<h2>` tag typically appears after it, and is much smaller. Although it is not shown in the image, there are additional headers you can add to a page (e.g., `<h3>`, `<h4>`, `<h5>`, and `<h6>`). Each header is subsequently smaller than the previous one.

Last Words about Headings

Headings are a great way to break up larger pieces of content to make it more manageable and easier to consume. Headers are critical for users and search engines alike.

Imagine how cumbersome it would be to read one long document. You'd probably be extremely confused and overwhelmed by the amount of information. You might not even read it at all! Without headings, it is difficult for users to quickly locate the information they need.

Now let's explore **Hyperlinks**.

Hyperlinks

If you recall from the *History of Search Engines* chapter, I mentioned that the World Wide Web was such a groundbreaking invention because it helped users better navigate and find information on the Internet by connecting webpages together with *Hyperlinks* (Wikipedia, n.d.).

Hyperlinks are also used by search engines crawlers to find new webpages to crawl and potentially index.

Here's an example of what a *link* looks like in HTML:

```
<a href="https://www.domainname.com/" /> Insert
Text Here </a>
```

As you can see the link is made up of the `<a>` *anchor tag* HTML element with an `href` *attribute*. `https://www.domainname.com/` is where the URL of the destination of the link is included.

And next comes the `Insert Text Here` which is used as a placeholder to show where the **Anchor Text** or clickable text that will be displayed.

Here's what the link looks like on the front-end of a website:

st getting started in SEO, you may want to read my SEO Specialist career guide for tips on how to learn SE

ersonal coaching, if you are interested, leave your name, and email in the contact form below, and I will fo

As you can see in the image, the anchor tag is highlighted and stands out from the rest of the text. Also in most cases, it is underlined. Again, the tag is clickable and will navigate to the destination URL.

While links may all look the same, they are not created equal or serve the same purpose for web admins and SEOs. Links fall into two categories: *Internal* and *External*.

Internal Links

Internal Links are links from one page on a website to another page on the same website (Moz, n.d.).

Think of the website as a house; an internal link is like stairs or a pathway to the backyard. These links help the searcher better navigate your webpage content.

Also, search engines can display internal links in the SERPs to save the searcher time by skipping to the part of your content that most likely answers their unique question. These are called "sitelinks" (Google Search Central, n.d.).

Internal links are generally used to help users navigate the site and help search engines crawl and understand the website's structure. In theory, search crawlers can more easily find and index the pages by better understanding the site structure.

External Links

External Links are links from one website's page to another website's page (Moz, n.d.).

If a website receives a link from another website, this is referred to as a ***Backlink*** or an *inbound link* (BacklinkO, n.d.).

Thinking back to our *house example,* external links would be "the road that gets you from one person's house to your house." External links are a *connection* from one website to another website.

The purpose of external links is to cite authoritative sources or to give credit to other websites for their ideas or content. For this reason, external links are also referred to as *editorial links*.

Last Words about Hyperlinks

Of all Tim Berners-Lee's inventions, Hyperlinks are arguably one of the most influential. Hyperlinks improve a website's usability, as well as its *visibility* on the Internet.

With so many different websites out there, many search engines have reported using links to help them find webpages easier. Again, this does not mean that having hyperlinks can improve ranking potential.

However, it makes sense that having a website with a clear internal linking structure and other related websites linking to it demonstrates to search engines that a website is easy to use. And we know that search engines and users value sites with a positive user experience.

Now for my final thoughts on On-Page SEO.

Final Words about On-Page SEO

In summary, On-Page SEO is all about making a website more appealing to users and search engines by optimizing the content on a website —the content being the information found in a website's HTML (HyperText Markup Language) code.

Improving the elements makes the content easier for both humans and search engines to read and understand.

Congratulations on making it through this part of the book as well. Did you find the on-page SEO section more concise and straightforward than technical SEO?

I recommend going through each on-page factor again and being in the habit of applying them to your website or someone else's website. This is one of the best ways to ensure the information you have learned is being used.

In the next chapter, we will explore the last and final domain of SEO, **Off-Page SEO**.

Off-Page SEO focuses on building a website's visibility and *authority* through gaining "backlinks" to a website from other websites on theirs.

We already discussed links in the *On-Page SEO* chapter, but we will explore links deeper in the following chapter. Let's get started.

Chapter 7: Off-Page SEO

Off-Page SEO, sometimes referred to as *Off-Site SEO* or *Link-Building*, is the domain of SEO that focuses on getting "backlinks" or other websites to link to a specific website or webpage (Silva, 2022).

Backlinks are prized by many SEO practitioners because they are believed to increase referral traffic or **PageRank**. You may also hear PageRank referred to as **"Link juice," "Link equity," "Ranking credit," or "Editorial votes."**

The term *Link juice* is rather informal; therefore, most professionals use the term PageRank.

At this point we have tossed around the term PageRank quite a bit - so, let's explore what it is and how it works.

PageRank

PageRank is the perceived trust from search engines that a webpage has; the term stems from Google's popular webpage ranking algorithm, *PageRank*.

Theoretically, gaining more backlinks means you are "increasing" PageRank, which may affect your ability to rank higher on SERPs.

The idea of gaining PageRank is influenced by the fine print from Google's patent: *Method for node ranking in a linked database* - this is a patent for the formula they use to decide how to rank websites on the search engine results page (SERP).

In the abstract it mentions that the method is based on Google (n.d.):

...The rank assigned to a document is calculated from the ranks of

documents citing it. In addition, the rank of a document is

calculated from a constant representing the probability that a

browser through the database will randomly jump to the document.

(para. 1)

Although Google's patent mentions citations are a factor they use when ranking pages, Google denies that Webmasters can influence this:

"I'd forget everything you read about "link juice." It's very likely all obsolete, wrong, and/or misleading. Instead, build a website that works well for your users" (John Mueller, Google Search Advocate, 2020).

The conflicting information from Google has led to some confusion in the SEO community. The question remains: *"Can link building improve your rankings or not?"*

Ultimately, there is no definite answer to the question above. For that reason, it can be best to think of link building as a way to build more brand awareness and authority on a subject, rather than just for the sake of improving PageRank.

Another Off-Page SEO factor that you will hear a lot about is **Domain Authority**.

Domain Authority

Domain Authority, also called **Thought Leadership,** is an SEO metric coined by the software company Moz. It is a way to gauge the likelihood a website will rank high on search engine results pages for its desired keywords.

Other companies have spoofed it into the term **Domain Rating,** but it is essentially the same metric. It is calculated from 0 - 100, with a higher score indicating a greater likelihood of ranking high on the SERPs (Wikipedia, n.d.).

Despite being a widely discussed metric in the SEO industry, it is not a factor that search engines use when determining which websites should rank for a particular search term. Moz has also confirmed that search engines don't use this metric (Moz, n.d.).

I have included this metric along with PageRank because many SEOs vouch for building backlinks with the intent to increase these two metrics.

But because there is no concrete evidence from search engines that backlinks affect a website's rankings, you could argue that these metrics may not be applicable or necessary. Nonetheless, they may still help you assess the overall relevance of your website in a particular niche.

In the next section, we will discuss some examples of methods that have been used to gain backlinks to a website.

Although there is no possible way to guarantee a page ranking boost from getting backlinks - that doesn't stop people from doing things to get links from other websites. So I want to advise you to use these methods at your own risk.

Common Link-Building Methods

As a professional in the SEO field, I have researched and even tried many of the link-building methods I will discuss in this section.

While there currently isn't any concrete evidence from search engines that these methods influence ranking potential. I think they are worth discussing and even researching on your own if you wish.

Link-Building Methods: Cold Email Outreach

The cold email outreach approach involves simply emailing the website owners that you want backlinks from and asking them to link to you.

This strategy has lost effectiveness over time, as website owners tend to be overwhelmed with requests that are in poor taste or irrelevant to their website.

Additionally, this approach is called "cold" because often, you do not already have an established relationship with the website owner you are requesting a link from.

In 2017, Authorityhackers conducted a study using an approach similar to cold outreach to gain backlinks. Their study mentioned that they sent out over 600,000 cold emails over a 3-year span to 150,000 website owners. The emails received a 53% open rate, and they got 4,306 backlinks (Ugor, 2022).

This study revealed that cold email could be an effective link-building strategy. My only critique is that it is a rather impersonal way of approaching link-building. Also, sending off that many emails at one time can get tedious and seem like spam. That's just my thoughts.

Link-Building Methods: Guest Blogging

Often website owners will explicitly ask for 3rd party bloggers to contribute to their blogs; this is called **Guest Blogging**.

Theoretically, this strategy works by "pitching" or recommending content to the blog owner; this pitch is either accepted or rejected. Pitches that get taken are generally the ones that blog owners feel are most valuable for their audience. If accepted, the blog owner will host your guest blog on their website.

Conversely, if your pitch gets rejected - that's no worries. You can take the same guest blog you created, and pitch it to a different blog owner.

In 2019 Adam Enfroy ran a 15-day guest blogging experiment. According to the 2019 study, Enfroy pitched posts to 68 website owners and received 28 responses. From those 28 responses, he published eight guest posts which resulted in 247 new backlinks and received a 372% increase in organic traffic (Enfroy, 2019).

Enfroy did mention that the initial outreach was through cold email, but overall it is more personal to offer value like a blog post rather than just a pitch.

Link-Building Methods: Help A Reporter Out

Help A Reporter Out, or HARO is a program the company Cision offers. In the program, journalists, news outlets, large publications, or website owners ask experts and other business owners to provide content they can use on their websites.

The program works by providing the subscriber with emails filled with "daily tips" or requests that other website owners want to be fulfilled.

In 2020, Johnathan Gorham conducted a study, and the findings revealed that he got 33 backlinks for his website from HARO (Gorham, 2020).

However, based on Jonathan's study, you have to have a strategy to get backlinks on HARO, and it takes time for the pitch to be accepted. Also, there is no guarantee of a response.

Link-Building Methods: PR / Earned media

Instead of using HARO to access news outlets, you can also try contacting them directly to get a placement - this is referred to as **Public Relations (PR)** or **Earned Media**.

Again, the idea is to offer or "pitch" content that is of value to them and their audience. So, with news outlets, this content can be local stories, proprietary research, expert opinions, or exclusive case studies.

Each outlet varies on what content they will and will not take, so it may be wise to research the outlet before reaching out.

In 2021, Domenica D'Ottavio conducted a case study on Moz. In the study, D'Ottavio explains how creating newsworthy content helped her gain 82 backlinks for her client in the home improvement niche.

D'Ottavio (2021) reports:

> Earned media is by far the most beneficial public relations tactic in
>
> 2021 and beyond. When you create data-backed content campaigns
>
> that provoke discussion in your industry, you also boost your brand
>
> awareness, trustworthiness, and rankings in the SERPS. It's a win-
>
> win-win tactic and will continue to take the lead when it comes to
>
> marketing tactics. (para. 40)

I think this quote by D'Ottavio highlights the importance of using link-building to build online authority as a whole, as opposed to just gaining ranking credit.

Link-Building Methods: Local Directories/Citations

A **Directory** is a website that compiles a list of businesses and their contact information. The website can do this automatically, but in some instances, a user is able to input their business information manually.

The listing or **Citation** for each business commonly includes their name, address, and phone number - this collection is referred to by the acronym **NAP (Name, Address, Phone Number)**.

Additionally, citations can include a business Website URL; because of this, many SEOs prioritize creating citations to build backlinks.

In 2016 BrightLocal conducted a study that found that 72% of local SEOs use citations as a way of building links (Marchant, 2016).

If that many SEOs use this tactic, it must be a relatively effective way to build links.

Link-Building Methods: Reclaiming Brand Mentions

There are instances where a business is mentioned on other websites without a link back to their website. In SEO, we call these **Unlinked Brand Mentions**.

Sometimes these unlinked mentions are intentional, as the website owner may have a policy prohibiting backlinking. It is best to check with each website owner to see if the unlinked brand mention can be claimed - and if a link to your website can be placed.

In a study conducted by Andrew Dennis (2018), he reported that he was able to get 64 backlinks for a client by using a combination of reclaiming brand mentions and competitive linking tactics (Dennis, 2018).

This study by Dennis highlights the effectiveness of this link-building tactic, but as I mentioned, this tactic can only work if the unlinked mentions are *unintentional*. Again, keep that in mind if you plan on trying out this tactic.

Link-Building Methods: Content Marketing

Content Marketing is a bit different from the other link-building methods; instead of asking for a backlink - you are essentially *attracting* links by producing content visitors "naturally" want to link to. Again, this content has to be valuable to prompt visitors to link to it.

In a 2014 case study by Brian Dean of BacklinkO, he utilized his unique content marketing method, the *Skyscraper Technique*.

Dean (2014) acquired 17 backlinks to his article on Google Ranking Factors through his method.

Dean (2014) reports:

> "Here's why this technique works so well (and what it has to do with a skyscraper):
>
> Have you ever walked by a really tall building and said to yourself:
>
> Wow, that's amazing! I wonder how big the 8th tallest building in the world is." Of course not. It's human nature to be attracted to the best. And what you're doing here is finding the tallest "skyscraper" in your space… and slapping 20 stories to the top of it. All of a sudden YOU have the content that everyone wants to talk about (and link to)." (para. 3)

The skyscraper method involves creating a piece of content significantly better than the highest ranking page for the keyword you are targeting, reaching out to website owners that link to the competitor content, and then asking them to link to you instead.

Dean appears to have had great success with this method. I've tried it a few times and heard it could be effective from my SEO friends. So it may be worth trying.

Link-Building Methods: Broken Link Building

Not to be confused with fixing 404 broken link errors on a website, **Broken Link-Building** is about finding sites with links to content similar to yours and then checking to see if any links are broken.

If there is a broken link, you can persuade the website owners to swap out the broken link with your content.

For this method to produce backlinks, the content you want to swap in typically needs to be of similar or more value.

SEO professional Sam Oh, also VP of Marketing at Ahrefs, ran a study where he sent out 74 outreach emails to web admins who had broken links. Four of the emails "bounced," meaning they didn't reach the webmaster at all. Five webmasters responded, but only one website gave Oh a link to their blog. Sam reported that this was a 1.4% conversion rate (Oh, 2021).

The strategy has lost popularity over the years. In Aira's 2022 *State of Link Building report*, they surveyed SEO professionals on what link-building strategies they use the most. Broken link-building is still in the top 5 link-building strategies used but is down to 39% from its peak of 53% in 2020 (Aira, 2022).

I've tried broken link building, and it honestly didn't work well for me. I found it hard to find pages with enough broken links.

Also, once you find a page, you still have to reach out to the webmaster to see if they are willing to swap out the broken link, which could take some time. That's just my experience, but it may still be worth trying.

Link-Building Methods: Social Media

Most social media websites allow users to create online profiles for business or personal use. With the business profile, you can often add a link to your website.

Additionally, by posting content to followers or subscribers, you can generate **"Social signals"** or repost of your content on social media websites. These social signals are similar to backlinks (Big Commerce, n.d.).

Similar to the concept of PageRank, Google denounces the idea of social signals. In 2021 when asked if website clicks via email affect rankings, Google Search advocate John Mueller stated:

"No effect on SEO. Like ads, like social media. It's good to have multiple separate sources of traffic to your website, and not everything needs to have an SEO effect" (Mueller, 2021).

Unfortunately, I could not find a reputable case study to prove the effectiveness of using social media for SEO purposes. Still, overall social media is helpful for building brand awareness and authority in general.

Link-Building Methods: Q & A Websites and Forums

Q & A websites allow users to ask questions and then field answers from other website users. Examples include Reddit, Quora, and StackOverflow.

Online forums are similar to Q & A sites except they are generally focused on one topic, whereas on Q & A websites, users can ask essentially any question.

SEOs often post on these websites with the intent to gain social signals as well, but similar to social media, Google does not consider these social signals when ranking pages.

Additionally, when researching this technique, there was a lack of case studies covering this method. Therefore, gaining backlinks via this method is anecdotal.

Link-Building Methods: Black Hat Link Building

While not the most ethical, there is a community of link builders that use methods to manipulate search engines to gain backlinks. These methods are known as **Black-Hat Link-Building**.

I wouldn't recommend using any of these methods, as Bounce Rank proudly practices and encourages using *White-Hat* SEO techniques only. However, it's important to be aware of black hat link building as it is prevalent.

One of the most common methods is creating *Private Blog Networks (PBNs)*, essentially a collection of websites created to build backlinks to a website.

Often these PBNs are against search engines' rules because the content placement is paid for, and the content of the PBNs is usually of poor quality and/or irrelevant to the backlink website.

According to Google Search Central (n.d.):

> Any links intended to manipulate PageRank or a site's ranking in
>
> Google search results may be considered part of a link scheme and
>
> a violation of Google's Webmaster Guidelines. This includes any
>
> behavior that manipulates links to your site or outgoing links from
>
> your site. (para. 18)

Other Black-Hat methods include:

- **Spamming**: adding unsolicited or poor taste links in other website owners' comments.
- **Cloaking**: serving one page of content to search engines, but serving a different page to users - which is again, often in poor taste. The cloaking webpage is usually filled with content that is not relevant to the backlinking website.

For the sake of your time and protection, I am not going to cite any case studies where users have tried using black-hat strategies. If you are curious, there are forums that explore this topic extensively, but again visit at your own risk.

Final Words about Off-Page SEO

There may be people who read this book with the expectation that I would go into exquisite detail about all the ways to build links and authority.

However, rather than explicitly instructing you on how to implement various backlink strategies - I believe what's more important is having a website optimized for users and letting other website owners know about it.

Now, I am certainly not one of those SEO professionals who say, *"Just make good content, and people will find it on their own."* However, I am proposing that you need a balance of strategy and quality content that you can exchange with website owners.

Often SEO practitioners rely heavily on backlinking because of its assumed ranking benefit - and they overlook the bigger picture, creating a healthy online reputation for your business.

Two points to take away from off-page SEO are:

1. You have to persuade a website owner to want to link back to you and that doesn't happen overnight. You have to build relationships with these website owners naturally.
2. The primary purpose of backlinks is to build your brand awareness and establish your website as an authority in your niche or industry.

I suggest starting with creating valuable content, then reaching out to website owners to boost it. In other words, there is no "conveyor belt-like" method for getting backlinks; it takes time and consistency.

Let's shift gears and explore how to collect and analyze **SEO KPIs (Key Performance Indicators)** to see if your strategies and practices are actually increasing a website's search ranking.

Chapter 8: Key Performance Indicators (KPIs)

A part of doing SEO, is you have to be able to tell if what you are doing is *actually* working. So let's talk about the best way to do that, and that is through tracking and analyzing **Key Performance Indicators (KPIs).**

By measuring *KPIs* you are able to make data-driven decisions and fix problems, if and when they arise (Wikipedia, n.d.).

In SEO, there are specific KPIs that can be used to measure the effectiveness of your strategy. The KPIs I am going to discuss in this section are the ones that are most commonly used by SEO beginners, and generally most relevant to business owners.

Here's the list of the KPIs I will be discussing in this chapter:

- Impressions
- Clicks
- Click Through Rate (CTR)
- Average Position
- Time On Page
- Bounce Rate
- Keyword Rankings
- Conversion Rate

You should understand each of these KPIs so you will be able to identify opportunities to improve a website. Learning these metrics will also help you share the data with others in your organization or, if you are an agency, with your clients.

Tracking these metrics can go a long way in helping you get more "buy-in" on future SEO projects and initiatives.

Okay, now let's explore each of these KPIs in detail.

Impressions

The number of times a user has seen (or potentially seen) a webpage in the search engine results is known as an **Impression**. It is counted every time the webpage is populated on the search engine results page, and not necessarily when the user scrolls to see it (Google Search Console Help, n.d.).

In theory, the more times a webpage is displayed, the more likely a user is to click on it and visit the website.

Clicks and Click Through Rate (CTR)

Clicks are the number of times a user has clicked on a webpage in the search engine results. **Click Through Rate** (**CTR**) is the number of times a user clicks on a website divided / by the number of impressions.

Here is the formula (Google Search Console Help, n.d.):

```
# of page clicks / # of page impressions = CTR%
```

Essentially having a higher number of clicks and a high CTR can indicate that the webpages' **Title Tag**, **Meta Description**, **URL**, and/or **keyword placement** *may* be engaging the user and convincing them to click on the website.

For example, a webpage with a CTR of 1.4% means that for every 1000 impressions, there are 14 clicks; the webpage is performing relatively well.

Average Position

The average placement a webpage has in the search engine results is measured by the metric **Average Position**. It is based on the topmost page or the high placement the page has received.

Search results pages differ based on the search query, so this metric is calculated based on the average position across all queries (Google Search Console Help, n.d.).

Generally, pages with a higher average position are deemed more trustworthy to search engines and thus are more likely to be clicked on.

Average Time On Page

Average Time On Page is an SEO KPI metric that measures how long a user spends on a specific page of a website (Google Search Ads 360 Help, n.d.). The metric is interchangeable with **Average Session Duration**.

It is recorded in minutes and seconds. According to Fultz (2022), it can be calculated by taking the **total amount of time spent on a page** and dividing / it by the **total number of non-page exits** and **bounces**.

Non-Page Exits are when a user leaves the page and goes to a different page on the website or another website altogether (Fultz, 2022).

A *Bounce* is when the user leaves the website to return to the search engine's results page (SERP) without visiting any other pages on the website (Fultz, 2022).

Here's an example equation:

```
20 minutes / (1000 pageviews - 500 page exits or
bounces) = 20/500 = 0.04 minutes or 2.4 seconds
average time on page
```

Average time on page is also a KPI used to measure a website's overall *User Experience (UX)* or how well the website can be used and accessed by all types of human users regardless of the different technical capabilities.

A poor time on page may indicate a poor UX. Users who do not quickly find what they seek on the page may leave the site and potentially bounce back to the SERPs.

Bounce Rate

Bounce Rate is a metric that measures the percentage of users that leave a website after visiting only one page.

According to Google Analytics Help (n.d.), bounce rate is calculated by taking the **total number of single-page sessions** divided / by **all sessions** or **the percentage of all sessions on your site** in which users viewed only a single page and triggered only a single request to the Analytics server.

Here's an example equation:

```
100 single-page sessions / 1000 total sessions =
10% bounce rate
```

Like time on page, bounce rate is another key indicator of a website's overall UX or how well the website can be used.

Keyword Rankings

Keyword rankings refer to a website's average position when it appears on the search engine results page for a specific keyword/search query. When identifying which queries a website ranks for the best, be aware that the lower the number, the better (Spinutech, 2018).

A lower number indicates that the website is ranking higher more frequently for that query, and vice versa. Think of it from the perspective of - we all want to be in the "number 1 spot."

Additionally, when determining the page that the website ranks for it is important to note that there are typically **10 organic listings** per search results page.

So when considering rankings, look at this sequence below (Spinutech, 2018):

Page 1: Rankings 1-10
Page 2: Rankings 11-20
Page 3: Rankings 21-30
Page 4: Rankings 31-40
Page 5: Rankings 41-50

One last thing to note about keyword rankings is that a website can and will show up at different positions for different keywords and search queries.

Therefore, when evaluating the overall search performance of a website, it is important to consider all possible keyword rankings to accurately determine the search performance of a website.

Conversion Rate

When someone comes to a website, the goal is for the visitor to share information (e.g., name, email, phone number, etc.) or make a purchase before leaving; this is called a **Conversion**.

For a local business, a conversion can be having an email list sign-up, a phone call, or a booked appointment (Moz, n.d.).

According to Searchmetrics (n.d.), the rate at which conversions happen is called the **Conversion Rate**. It is calculated by taking the **number of conversions** and dividing / it by **the number of visitors.**

Here is the formula:

```
10 conversions / 1000 visitors = 1% conversion
rate
```

For every business, the desired conversion rate will be different, but across industries, the average conversion rate is 2.35% (Kim, 2022).

How to Analyze and Present SEO Data

Now that I went over each of the different SEO KPIs to track, I want to follow-up with a discussion on how to analyze SEO data.

This is my account of how I analyze data and then present it to my clients, but I also included references to other articles that discuss the same topic.

The simplest way to analyze data is to look for metrics where you see underperformance and compare it to another KPI or to where the metric has been in the past (i.e., a benchmark).

Let's explore some common scenarios:

KPI Scenarios: Low Clicks but High Impressions

Having a low amount of webpage clicks but high impressions may indicate that the webpage is either:

- Not ranking on page 1 yet for its intended keywords.
- The page's Title Tag, Meta Description, or URL is not enticing to the user.

As you can already see, with data analysis, there is not one clear reason why you do not see the results you wish.

Because your results could be more apparent, digging deeper into the data and finding the root cause of why a metric is not meeting your expectations is essential.

For instance: let's imagine you're not ranking on page 1 for your target keywords. This might not be the end of the world.

Brian Dean conducted a case study in 2022; he analyzed over 4 million Google search results, and he found that:

"Only 0.78% of Google search engine users clicked on something from the second page" (BacklinkO, 2022).

And the CTR decreased significantly as you move to pages three, four, and beyond.

In other words, not ranking on page 1 is not necessarily a bad thing in the beginning, because it could indicate that the webpage may need more time to rank on page 1.

Conversely, if you have been targeting a particular keyword for a substantial amount of time and you aren't seeing any improvement in rankings, this could be a cause for concern.

In a nutshell, if you have low clicks but high impressions and you're not ranking on page one - it could mean your webpage is appearing on the SERPs (high impressions) but it isn't ranking high enough yet (low clicks).

Now let's imagine you are seeing low clicks and high impressions but your webpage is on page 1 - then your issue may be that the webpage's, *Title Tag, Meta Description, or URL is not enticing enough to the user.*

To once again cite statistics from Brian Dean's (2022) study, he found that:

"Title tags between 40 to 60 characters have the highest CTR" and "URLs that contain terms similar to a keyword have a 45% higher click-through rate compared to URLs that don't contain a keyword" (BacklinkO, 2022).

In this instance, you may want to try *A/B split Testing*, which is when you have two variations of each of these elements, and you test to see which one is the most enticing for users (i.e. get the most clicks) (Costello, 2020).

Alternatively, viewing competitor pages to see how they have written their HTML elements may be wise. You can get some ideas on what formats and content work best.

As with all data analysis, you want to monitor the data to see how things progress and make adjustments over time.

KPI Scenarios: High Clicks but Low Time On Page or High Bounce Rate

In my experience, when you have a high number of webpage clicks, but users are not staying on the page for long, this usually indicates that users either:

- Found the answer that they were looking for and just happened to leave prematurely.
- Were not able to navigate the webpage well (user experience issues).

In the case of the first potential reason, this may be a good thing, in Google's Analytics Help documentation (n.d.) for *Bounce Rate*, they mention that:

"If you have a single-page site like a blog, or offer other types of content for which single-page sessions are expected, then a high bounce rate is perfectly normal." (Google Analytics Help, n.d.)

This makes sense that most users are would prefer a webpage that provides them an answer to their problem relatively quickly (hence the high clicks).

However, for web admins whose website success is contingent on users visiting more than one page, especially business owners, this is likely an issue with the webpages' overall quality.

According to Google Analytics Help (n.d.):

> If the success of your site depends on users viewing more than one
> page, then, yes, a high bounce rate is bad. For example, if your
> home page is the gateway to the rest of your site (e.g., news
> articles, product pages, your checkout process) and a high
> percentage of users are viewing only your home page, then you
> don't want a high bounce rate. (para. 4)

In my experience, a page could be considered low quality due to:

- Having conflicting font colors and theme colors
- Font that is too small
- Font style that is hard to read
- The page has distracting pop up ads
- The webpage had a soft 404 (the page is blank)
- 500 or 503 server response code leading to a page being unable to
  be loaded

A variety of things can lead to a poor user experience. Some things
are in your control, and others are not. It is best to analyze the whole
quality of the page to see if it is a user experience issue.

This scenario perfectly exemplifies how "context" is essential
when analyzing and reporting data. When interpreting and sharing data,
context is everything.

In conclusion, high clicks with a low time on page or bounce rate
is not alarming if you're talking about a blog post - but it can be
concerning if you're an eCommerce store, for instance. Context matters.

KPI Scenarios: Low Click-Through Rate (1% > X)

Similar to having low clicks, if a webpage's CTR (click-through rate) is low as well, this may also indicate that:

- The Title Tag, Meta Description, or URL is not enticing enough to searchers.
- The webpage has not yet reached page 1 for its keywords.

When this scenario arises, it is best to examine the number of clicks and impressions over time before making changes to your tags or changing the webpage in general.

Last Words about Key Performance Indicators (KPIs)

In this chapter, we explored examples of common SEO metrics worth tracking; there are many other KPIs that you can assess and track. But in general, tracking impressions, clicks, CTR, keyword rankings, and conversion rate is enough to see if your SEO efforts are paying off.

Of course, naturally, there will be times when it just seems like nothing is working, and that can be frustrating.

What I would like you to take away from this chapter is that; it is vital to consider all possible reasons or scenarios for why you may not see the desired results. Also, SEO requires patience and time to see results.

As you can see from the scenarios we went over, sometimes the culprit is that the webpage needs more time to rank. That is important to consider because SEO is a long-term strategy and should be treated as such.

Another thing to keep in mind while analyzing your data, the results you're seeing do not always indicate that you are doing something "wrong." Again, your webpage may need more time to rank.

Although SEO takes time, you can still see meaningful improvements, even if it's just a few more clicks or impressions daily.

I hope you found this chapter valuable for learning how to analyze your SEO data. By accurately assessing your current standings, you will soon find it easier to make informed decisions that, with time, can multiply your SEO efforts.

Thank you for making it to the end of the book. In the last section I will make my closing remarks and tell you how you can best go about applying what you have learned!

Closing Remarks

Congratulations on making it to the end of the book! After writing this book, I hope I have given you more than enough direction, strategy, and knowledge to apply Search Engine Optimization in a higher-level manner.

I also hope that the knowledge you have gained will help you to make genuinely impactful changes to any website that you may be working on.

As you continue to learn SEO, you may discover that some of the information you come across may not be applicable anymore. For this reason, I designed this book to be a timeless resource for you no matter where you go in your journey.

My recommendation is to go back through the book, find any topics or ideas you feel fuzzy about, take that information, and look it up on your favorite search engine.

Please cross-reference the information you read here with other readings you find. Doing so will help you gain an even more holistic understanding of how the SEO process works.

One last thing I want to leave you with is that you will have moments where you feel like, no matter what you do, you can't understand how SEO works. But rest assured -that's okay!

It has taken me nearly a decade to perform SEO at a high level and explain it in an easy-to-understand manner that anyone can comprehend.

Just as Rome wasn't built in a day - you most likely will not learn SEO in a day either. It would behoove you to take your time and practice these concepts as much as possible. Before you know it, you'll be able to make impactful changes and gain robust and long-term SEO results.

Thank you again for reading this book, and I wish you the best of luck on your SEO journey and in life in general.

Kind regards,

Raj Clark

Glossary

200 (OK) - A server response code indicating that the server is functioning properly and is ready to process the next request from the client.

301 (Moved Permanently) - A server response code indicating that the content has been permanently moved to a new location on the website.

307 (Temporary Redirect) - A server response code indicating that the content has been temporarily moved to a new location on the website.

404 (Not Found) - A server response code indicating that the content could not be found on the website.

500 (Internal Server Error) - A server response code indicating that there was a problem with accessing the website. This could be a Web hosting issue.

503 (Service Unavailable) - A server response code indicating that the website is unavailable. This could be a Web hosting issue.

Algorithm - The set of rules used by a search engine to determine what webpages are relevant to a particular query or search term.

Allow Rule - A request formatted in the Robots.txt file that specifies to search engines spiders to crawl a particular directory.

Average Position - The average position of a website in the organic results for a particular keyword or phrase.

Backlinks - Links from one website to another. May be used by search engines to determine the popularity of particular webpages.

Bounce Rate - A measure of the percentage of visitors who enter a website and then leave without clicking on any other pages.

Canonical Tag - A tag that tells search engines that a particular page is the original version of a webpage and not a duplicate.

Click Through Rate (CTR) - The ratio of visitors who click on a search result to the number of times the result was displayed.

Clicks - The number of times a webpage is clicked on in search results.

CLS - Cumulative Layout Shift - A metric coined by Google that measures how much the layout of a webpage shifts when it is initially loaded and when it is in use.

Competition Score - A measure of how many links are pointing to a particular website, or how difficult it will be to rank for a particular keyword.

Conversion Rate - The percentage of visitors who perform the desired action, like making a purchase, filling out a form or signing up for a service.

Core Updates - A set of major updates Google makes to its search engine algorithms that have a significant impact on ranking of websites in its search results.

Core Web Vitals - A set of metrics that Google uses to measure a website overall user experience, speed and performance.

Crawling - The process of a search engine spider or bot visiting a website to find and index new content.

Disallow Rule - A rule in the robots.txt file that tells search engines not to crawl a specific directory or folder on a website.

Domain Authority - A score created by the software company; Moz used to assess the authority of a website or the likelihood of a domain to rank well in search results.

Domain Naming System (DNS) - A system that connects domain names to IP addresses.

Duplicate Content - Webpage content that appears on multiple URLs on the same or different websites.

E-E-A-T - An acronym coined by Google; Experience, Expertise, Authoritativeness, and Trust are four metrics used by Google to determine the quality of a website and it's worthiness for inclusion in their search results.

External Links - A hyperlink on one website that links to another website.

FID - First Input Delay - A term coined by Google, the time it takes for a user to begin interacting with a website after it has loaded.

File Transfer Protocol (FTP) - A network protocol that allows files to be delivered to a web server.

Geotags - A type of keyword that targets a specific geographic location.

Google - Google Inc, a subsidiary of Alphabet Inc., is an American multinational technology company founded by Sergey Brin and Larry Page. That is popular for their search engine and advertising technologies.

Headers (H1, H2, H3, H4, H5 and H6) - Headers are the HTML tags that determine the hierarchy of a webpage.

Hreflang Tag - A type of HTML tag that is used to specify a language for a page on a multilingual website.

HTML (HyperText Markup Language) - HyperText Markup Language is a coding language pioneered by Tim Berners-Lee, it is used to create webpages and web applications.

Hyperlinks - A clickable element on a webpage that directs the user to another webpage or a different section of the same webpage.

HyperText Transfer Protocol (HTTP) - It is the underlying protocol used for transferring data on the World Wide Web. It is a client-server protocol, which means that requests are initiated by the recipient, usually the web browser.

HyperText Transfer Protocol Secure (HTTPS) - It is a secure version of the HTTP protocol that uses encryption to ensure that data transmitted between the client and the server cannot be intercepted or tampered with by third parties.

Image Alt Text - It is an attribute added to an HTML image tag that provides a description of the image for those who cannot see the image or for search engine crawlers.

Impressions -It refers to the number of times a specific piece of content, such as an ad or a webpage, has been displayed to a user.

Index - It refers to a database of webpages or other content that search engines use to find relevant results for user queries.

Indexing - It is the process by which search engines crawl and analyze webpages to add them to their index.

Internal Links - They are hyperlinks that connect one page of a website to another page on the same website.

Key Performance Indicators (KPIs) - They are specific metrics used to measure the success of a business or website. KPIs can be used to track progress towards goals and objectives.

Keyword Rankings - They refer to the position of a website in the search engine results pages (SERPs) for a particular keyword or search query.

Keyword Research - It is the process of identifying and analyzing keywords and phrases that people use to search for information on the internet.

Keywords -They are words or phrases that can be included on a webpage to help it appear for related queries.

LCP - Largest Contentful Paint - It is a metric used to measure the loading performance of a webpage. It refers to the time it takes for the largest element on a webpage to load.

Link-Building - It is the process of acquiring links from other websites to improve the search engine rankings of a website.

Long-Tail Keyword - It is a keyword or phrase that is more specific and less commonly searched for than a general keyword. They are often used to target audiences that are more likely to convert.

Meta Descriptions - They are HTML tags that provide a brief summary of the content of a webpage. They are often displayed in the search engine results pages (SERPs) as a preview of the webpage.

Nested - It refers to an HTML element or object that is contained within another element or object.

Noindex Meta Tag - It is an HTML tag that instructs search engines not to include a webpage in their index.

Off-Page SEO - It refers to the optimization of a website's online presence outside of its own webpages. This includes activities such as public relations and social media marketing.

On-Page SEO - It refers to the optimization of a website's own webpages to improve search engine rankings. This includes activities such as optimizing content, titles, and meta descriptions, as well as improving website structure and usability.

PageRank: The perceived trust that a webpage or website has based on the number of editorial votes it receives. There is no concrete evidence from Google, that this metric exists and that it can be influenced.

Queries - These are the questions or search terms that a user inputs into a search engine in order to find information.

Ranking Factors - These are the various factors that search engines consider when determining the order in which websites are displayed in search results.

Rendering - Refers to the process of a web browser turning HTML, CSS, and JavaScript code into a visual representation of a website.

Robots.txt File - This is a file that website owners can create to instruct search engine crawlers which pages of their website to crawl and index.

Schema Markup - A type of microdata that website owners can use to help search engines understand the content of their webpages.

Search Bar - This is a text box on a website or search engine where users can input search queries.

Search Engine Results Page (SERPs) - This is the page that a search engine displays after a user inputs a search query. It shows a list of websites that the search engine has determined to be relevant to the query.

Search Engines -These are websites that allow users to search the internet for information by entering search queries.

Search Intent - This refers to the underlying goal or purpose behind a user's search query. Understanding search intent is important for optimizing content to meet users' needs.

Search Volume - This is the number of searches that are conducted for a particular keyword or search term over a given period of time.

Second Level Domain (SLD) - This is the part of a website's domain name that comes immediately after the top-level domain (TLD). For example, in the domain name example.com, "example" is the SLD.

Seed Keyword - This is the starting point for keyword research, usually a word or phrase that is related to the topic or content of a website.

SEO - Search engine optimization (SEO) is the practice of optimizing a website's content and structure to improve its visibility and ranking in search engine results.

Server - A server is a computer or system that hosts websites and delivers them to users when they access the site.

Server Response Codes - These are codes that a server sends back to a browser to indicate the status of a requested webpage. Examples include 200 (OK), 404 (Not Found), and 500 (Internal Server Error).

Short-Tail Keyword - A keyword composed of only one or two words and are more general in nature. Because of their broadness, the search intent behind them is not always clear. As a result, they're more competitive than long-tail keywords, but tend to have a higher search volume.

Sitemap Reference - This is a link to a sitemap in the Robots.txt file

Slug - In web design, a slug refers to the part of a URL that identifies a specific page on a website.

Spiders - These are automated programs that search engines use to crawl the web and collect information about websites.

Subdirectory - This is a folder on a website that contains additional pages and content, organized under a main category or topic.

Subdomain - A subdomain is a separate part of a website that is treated as a separate entity by search engines. It typically has its own unique URL.

Technical SEO - This refers to the practice of optimizing a website's technical structure and elements to improve its search engine visibility. This can include optimizing a Robots.txt file, XML Sitemap, adding Meta tags and improving the website's load time.

Time On Page - This is the amount of time that a user spends on a particular webpage before navigating away or clicking through to another page. The term is comparable to Average session duration.

Title Tags - An HTML tag that appears in the header of a webpage and provides a brief description of the page's topic or focus. It also may be used by search engines as a ranking factor.

Top Level Domain (TLD): This is the last part of a website's domain name, examples include .com, .org, or .net

Uniform Resource Locators (URLs) - The unique addresses that identify specific webpages on the internet. They consist of several parts, including the protocol (e.g., http or https), the domain name (e.g., www.example.com), and any additional path or query parameters that specify the specific resource being requested.

User Experience (UX) - Refers to the overall quality of interaction that a person has with a website or digital product. It encompasses all aspects of the user's experience, including the ease of use, the accessibility of information, and the overall satisfaction of the user.

User-Agent - A directive defined in the Robots.txt files that specifies which search crawlers are allowed or not allowed to crawl a website.

Web Crawlers - Web crawlers, also known as spiders or bots, are automated software programs that scan and index the content of websites.

They are used by search engines to gather information about the content of webpages and to build an index of the internet.

Web Hosting - Refers to the service of providing server space and bandwidth to host websites on the internet. It allows individuals and organizations to make their websites accessible to the public.
Webmaster - A person responsible for managing and maintaining a website. They are typically responsible for ensuring that the website is up-to-date, secure, and functioning properly.

World Wide Web - The World Wide Web (WWW) is a system of interconnected documents and resources, accessed via the internet. It was invented by Tim Berners-Lee in 1989 and has since become a primary means of communication and information exchange on the internet.

XML Sitemaps - A file that lists all the pages on a website and provides information about their relationships and priority. They are used by search engines to crawl and index the content of a website more efficiently.

References

Adam, T. (2008, April 21). *The Art of SEO Evangelism*. Tony Adam.

Retrieved December 24, 2022, from https://tonyadam.com/the-art-

of-seo-evangelism/

Ahrefs. (n.d.). *What is a Noindex Tag?* Ahrefs. Retrieved December 3,

2022, from https://ahrefs.com/seo/glossary/noindex-tag

Aira. (2022). *Link Building Techniques and Tools*. Aira. Retrieved

December 22, 2022, from https://aira.net/state-of-link-

building/link-building-techniques-and-tools/

Avira. (n.d.). *What does error 500/503 mean? – Official Avira Support |*

Knowledgebase & Customer Support | Avira. Official Avira

Support. Retrieved December 5, 2022, from

https://support.avira.com/hc/en-us/articles/360000793305-What-

does-error-500-503-mean-

BacklinkO. (n.d.). *Core Web Vitals: What They Are & How to Improve*

Them. Backlinko. Retrieved December 4, 2022, from

https://backlinko.com/hub/seo/core-web-vitals

BacklinkO. (n.d.). *Duplicate Content and SEO: The Complete Guide*.

Backlinko. Retrieved December 31, 2022, from

https://backlinko.com/hub/seo/duplicate-content

BacklinkO. (n.d.). *What are Backlinks? And How to Build Them in 2021*. Backlinko. Retrieved December 14, 2022, from https://backlinko.com/hub/seo/backlinks

Baggan, E. (2021, February 2). *How seasonal SERP changes affect SEO*. OnCrawl. Retrieved December 28, 2022, from https://www.oncrawl.com/technical-seo/seasonal-serp-changes-seo/

Baker, K. (2021, February 12). *What's a Subdomain & How Is It Used?* HubSpot Blog. Retrieved December 5, 2022, from https://blog.hubspot.com/website/what-is-a-subdomain

BigCommerce. (n.d.). *What are social signals? How social media impacts SEO*. BigCommerce. Retrieved December 22, 2022, from https://www.bigcommerce.com/ecommerce-answers/what-are-social-signals/

BrightEdge. (n.d.). *Organic Search Improves Ability to Map to Consumer Intent:*. BrightEdge. Retrieved April 16, 2023, from https://videos.brightedge.com/research-report/BrightEdge_ChannelReport2019_FINAL.pdf

Brittanica. (n.d.). *Computer programming language - Visual Basic | Britannica*. Encyclopedia Britannica. Retrieved April 1, 2023, from https://www.britannica.com/technology/computer-

programming-language/Visual-Basic#ref849838

Brockbank, J. (2012, October 29). *Losing Paradise*. Semrush. Retrieved

December 5, 2022, from

https://www.semrush.com/blog/subdomain-vs-subdirectory/

Bruemmer, P. (2011, December 29). *How To Get A 30% Increase In CTR*

With Structured Markup. Search Engine Land. Retrieved

December 5, 2022, from https://searchengineland.com/how-to-get-

a-30-increase-in-ctr-with-structured-markup-105830

Caren, J. (2021, June 3). *Robots.txt: The Deceptively Important File All*

Websites Need. HubSpot Blog. Retrieved December 2, 2022, from

https://blog.hubspot.com/marketing/robots-txt-file

Chrome Developers. (2019, May 2). *Time to Interactive*. Chrome

Developers. Retrieved December 7, 2022, from

https://developer.chrome.com/en/docs/lighthouse/performance/inte

ractive/

Computer Hope. (2017, November 10). *What is a Domain?* Computer

Hope. Retrieved December 31, 2022, from

https://www.computerhope.com/jargon/d/domain.htm

Content King. (2021, October 12). *Robots.txt for SEO: Create the Best one With This 2021 Guide*. ContentKing. Retrieved April 2, 2023, from https://www.contentkingapp.com/academy/robotstxt/

Costello, R. (2020, May 7). *A/B & Multivariate Testing for SEO: How to Do It the Right Way*. Search Engine Journal. Retrieved December 28, 2022, from https://www.searchenginejournal.com/a-b-multivariate-testing-seo/366184/#close

Crestodina, A. (n.d.). *Search vs. Social: 9 Differences Between SEO and Social Media*. Orbit Media. Retrieved April 16, 2023, from https://www.orbitmedia.com/blog/social-media-seo/

Dean, B. (n.d.). *Search Intent and SEO: A Complete Guide*. Backlinko. Retrieved November 30, 2022, from https://backlinko.com/hub/seo/search-intent

Dean, B. (2021, October 10). *Google's 200 Ranking Factors: The Complete List (2022)*. Backlinko. Retrieved November 30, 2022, from https://backlinko.com/google-ranking-factors

Dean, B. (2022, February 26). *Link Building Case Study: How I Increased My Search Traffic by 110% in 14 Days*. Backlinko. Retrieved December 18, 2022, from https://backlinko.com/skyscraper-technique

Dean, B. (2022, October 14). *We Analyzed 4 Million Google Search Results. Here's What We Learned About Organic CTR*. Backlinko. Retrieved December 28, 2022, from https://backlinko.com/google-ctr-stats

Dennis, A. (2018, February 14). *A link-building case study: Using brand mentions and competitive linking tactics*. Search Engine Land. Retrieved December 18, 2022, from https://searchengineland.com/a-link-building-case-study-using-brand-mentions-and-competitive-linking-tactics-290048

De Valk, J. (2022, March 1). *hreflang: the ultimate guide • Yoast - Multilingual SEO*. Yoast. Retrieved December 4, 2022, from https://yoast.com/hreflang-ultimate-guide/

Doglio, F. (2020, August 12). *The JIT in JavaScript: Just In Time Compiler*. Bits and Pieces. Retrieved December 9, 2022, from https://blog.bitsrc.io/the-jit-in-javascript-just-in-time-compiler-798b66e44143

Donahole, S. (2020, November 17). *How Does My Hosting Provider Affect Site Speed*. Medium. Retrieved December 5, 2022, from https://medium.com/cornertechandmarketing/how-does-my-hosting-provider-affect-site-speed-1e05c4d98e7f

D'Ottavio, D. (2021, April 8). *Earn Press Coverage for Your Brand in 5 Steps [Case Study]*. Moz. Retrieved December 18, 2022, from https://moz.com/blog/five-steps-to-earn-press-coverage

DYNO Mapper. (n.d.). *About XML Sitemaps*. DYNO Mapper. Retrieved December 3, 2022, from https://dynomapper.com/sitemaps/amp

Eaton, B. (2022, August 19). *Web Crawlers - Top 10 Most Popular*. KeyCDN. Retrieved December 2, 2022, from https://www.keycdn.com/blog/web-crawlers

Edwards, B. (2021, August 24). *The Web Before the Web: A Look Back at Gopher*. How-To Geek. Retrieved December 7, 2022, from https://www.howtogeek.com/661871/the-web-before-the-web-a-look-back-at-gopher/

Eich, B., & Dahl, R. (n.d.). *JavaScript*. Wikipedia. Retrieved December 8, 2022, from https://en.wikipedia.org/wiki/JavaScript

Enfroy, A. (2019). *Guest Blogging in 2023: How I Wrote 80+ Guest Posts in 1 Year*. Adam Enfroy. Retrieved December 18, 2022, from https://www.adamenfroy.com/guest-blogging

Fitzgerald, A. (2020, December 28). *13 Tips for Choosing the Perfect Domain Name*. HubSpot Blog. Retrieved December 31, 2022, from https://blog.hubspot.com/website/how-to-choose-domain-name

Fultz, J. D. (2022, August 29). *What Is Average Time on Page and How to Increase It*. OptinMonster. Retrieved December 24, 2022, from https://optinmonster.com/how-to-increase-average-time-on-page/

Google. (n.d.). *Shopping research before purchase statistics*. Think with Google. Retrieved April 16, 2023, from https://www.thinkwithgoogle.com/consumer-insights/consumer-trends/shopping-research-before-purchase-statistics/

Google Developers. (2022, September 2). *Link text | Google developer documentation style guide*. Google Developers. Retrieved December 15, 2022, from https://developers.google.com/style/link-text

Google Search Ads 360 Help. (n.d.). *GA avg time on page column - Search Ads 360 Help*. Google Support. Retrieved December 24, 2022, from https://support.google.com/searchads/answer/6125075?hl=en

Google Search Central. (n.d.). *//. //* - Wikipedia. Retrieved December 22, 2022, from https://developers.google.com/search/docs/essentials/spam-policies?hl=en&visit_id=638072933577621689-1687435312&rd=1#link-spam

Google Search Central. (n.d.). *Consolidate Duplicate URLs with Canonical Tags | Google Search Central | Documentation*. Google Developers. Retrieved December 3, 2022, from https://developers.google.com/search/docs/crawling-indexing/consolidate-duplicate-urls

Google Search Central. (n.d.). *Core Web Vitals report - Search Console Help*. Google Support. Retrieved December 4, 2022, from https://support.google.com/webmasters/answer/9205520?hl=en

Google Search Central. (n.d.). *Core Web Vitals report - Search Console Help*. Google Support. Retrieved December 4, 2022, from https://support.google.com/webmasters/answer/9205520?hl=en

Google Search Central. (n.d.). *Crawl Budget Management For Large Sites | Google Search Central | Documentation*. Google Developers. Retrieved December 28, 2022, from https://developers.google.com/search/docs/crawling-indexing/large-site-managing-crawl-budget

Google Search Central. (n.d.). *Google URL Structure Guidelines | Google Search Central | Documentation*. Google Developers. Retrieved March 19, 2023, from https://developers.google.com/search/docs/crawling-indexing/url-structure

Google Search Central. (n.d.). *Headings and titles | Google developer documentation style guide*. Google Developers. Retrieved April 4, 2023, from https://developers.google.com/style/headings

Google Search Central. (n.d.). *Home*. YouTube. Retrieved April 22, 2023, from https://www.youtube.com/watch?v=Vej7f43fiyM&t=1903s

Google Search Central. (n.d.). *How to Write Meta Descriptions | Google Search Central | Documentation*. Google Developers. Retrieved December 14, 2022, from

https://developers.google.com/search/docs/appearance/snippet

Google Search Central. (n.d.). *How to Write Meta Descriptions | Google Search Central | Documentation*. Google Developers. Retrieved December 15, 2022, from

https://developers.google.com/search/docs/appearance/snippet

Google Search Central. (n.d.). *In-Depth Guide to How Google Search Works | Google Search Central | Documentation*. Google Developers. Retrieved December 12, 2022, from https://developers.google.com/search/docs/fundamentals/how-search-works

Google Search Central. (n.d.). *Influencing Title Links in Google Search | Google Search Central | Documentation*. Google Developers.

Retrieved December 15, 2022, from

https://developers.google.com/search/docs/appearance/title-link

Google Search Central. (n.d.). *Learn About What Sitelinks Are | Google Search Central | Documentation.* Google Developers. Retrieved December 14, 2022, from

https://developers.google.com/search/docs/appearance/sitelinks

Google Search Central. (n.d.). *What Is a Sitemap | Google Search Central | Documentation.* Google Developers. Retrieved December 3, 2022, from https://developers.google.com/search/docs/crawling-indexing/sitemaps/overview

Google Search Central. (2017, December 21). *Subdomain or subfolder, which is better for SEO?* YouTube. Retrieved December 5, 2022, from https://www.youtube.com/watch?v=uJGDyAN9g-g&feature=emb_title

Google Search Central. (2020, July 11). *English Google Webmaster Central office-hours from September 27, 2019.* YouTube. Retrieved December 14, 2022, from

https://www.youtube.com/watch?v=rwpwq8Ynf7s&t=1427s

Google Search Central. (2022, August 23). *Structured data for web developers | Search Central Lightning Talks.* YouTube. Retrieved

Decemeber 5, 2022, from

https://www.youtube.com/watch?v=hUHjeDylhE8&t=65s

Google Search Central. (2022, 11). *Robots.txt Introduction and Guide |*

Google Search Central | Documentation. Google Developers.

Retrieved December 2, 2022, from

https://developers.google.com/search/docs/crawling-

indexing/robots/intro

Google Search Central. (2023, 2). *Block Search Indexing with noindex |*

Google Search Central | Documentation. Google Developers.

Retrieved March 24, 2023, from

https://developers.google.com/search/docs/crawling-

indexing/block-indexing

Google Search CentralSe. (n.d.). *Google Image SEO Best Practices |*

Google Search Central | Documentation. Google Developers.

Retrieved December 15, 2022, from

https://developers.google.com/search/docs/appearance/google-

images

Google Search Console Help. (n.d.). *Manual Actions report - Search*

Console Help. Google Support. Retrieved December 23, 2022,

from

https://support.google.com/webmasters/answer/9044175?hl=en#zi

ppy=%2Cunnatural-links-to-your-site

Google Search Console Help. (n.d.). *What are impressions, position, and*

clicks? - Search Console Help. Google Support. Retrieved

December 24, 2022, from

https://support.google.com/webmasters/answer/7042828?hl=en#im

pressions

Google Support. (n.d.). *Indexing - Search Console Help*. Google Support.

Retrieved December 2, 2022, from

https://support.google.com/webmasters/answer/7645831?hl=en

Gorham, J. (2020, August 12). *HARO Link Building Case Study: How I*

Built 33 Links In 6 Hours. Engine Scout. Retrieved December 18,

2022, from https://enginescout.com.au/10-minute-backlinks/

Gotch, N. (2022, October 2). *How to Start an SEO Business in 2022 (A-Z*

Process). Gotch SEO. Retrieved December 30, 2022, from

https://www.gotchseo.com/start-seo-company/

Hall, M. (2022, November 3). *Google | History & Facts | Britannica*.

Encyclopedia Britannica. Retrieved December 7, 2022, from

https://www.britannica.com/topic/Google-Inc

Hardwick, J. (2022, May 23). *Broken Link Building: The Complete Guide.* Ahrefs. Retrieved December 22, 2022, from https://ahrefs.com/blog/broken-link-building/

Hardwick, J., & Mueller, J. (2020, April 14). *Canonical Tags: A Simple Guide for Beginners.* Ahrefs. Retrieved December 28, 2022, from https://ahrefs.com/blog/canonical-tags/

Harvard University. (n.d.). *Write good Alt Text to describe images.* Harvard's Digital Accessibility Services. Retrieved December 14, 2022, from https://accessibility.huit.harvard.edu/describe-content-images

Haverbeke, M. (2018). *Values, Types, and Operators.* Eloquent JavaScript. Retrieved March 27, 2023, from https://eloquentjavascript.net/01_values.html

Headings and titles | Google developer documentation style guide. (2022, August 5). Google Developers. Retrieved December 14, 2022, from https://developers.google.com/style/headings

Hendriks, M. (2022, August 11). *What is an XML sitemap and why should you have one?* Yoast. Retrieved December 3, 2022, from https://yoast.com/what-is-an-xml-sitemap-and-why-should-you-have-one/

Hlopov, N. (2021, May 19). *How to include CSS to a page (with Pros and Cons)*. Nikita Hlopov. Retrieved December 9, 2022, from https://nikitahl.com/how-to-include-css-to-a-page

Hoffmann, J. (2017, October 22). *A Look Back at the History of CSS | CSS-Tricks*. CSS-Tricks. Retrieved December 8, 2022, from https://css-tricks.com/look-back-history-css/

Holmes, T. (2022, December 1). *What is a Subdirectory? (with pictures)*. EasyTechJunkie. Retrieved December 5, 2022, from https://www.easytechjunkie.com/what-is-a-subdirectory.htm

IBM. (n.d.). *Home*. YouTube. Retrieved December 9, 2022, from https://www.ibm.com/docs/en/zos/2.1.0?topic=program-string-values

Indig, K. (2022, February 7). *What Is Technical SEO? Your Guide to Getting Started*. SEMrush. Retrieved November 30, 2022, from https://www.semrush.com/blog/learning-technical-seo/

JavaScript Basics (2022 Tutorial & Examples). (n.d.). BrainStation. Retrieved December 9, 2022, from https://brainstation.io/learn/javascript/basics

K, V. (2021, October 1). *JavaScript : Advantages and disadvantages of External JavaScript ?* scmGalaxy. Retrieved December 9, 2022, from https://www.scmgalaxy.com/tutorials/javascript-advantages-and-disadvantages-of-external-javascript/

Kim, L. (2022, November 12). *What Is a Good Conversion Rate? It's Higher Than You Think!* WordStream. Retrieved December 27, 2022, from

https://www.wordstream.com/blog/ws/2014/03/17/what-is-a-good-conversion-rate

Krishnan, J., & Chang, W.-T. (2021, June 7). *Using AVIF to compress images on your site*. web.dev. Retrieved December 12, 2022, from https://web.dev/compress-images-avif/

Lahey, C. (2021, March 30). *History of the Most Important Google Algorithm Updates*. Semrush. Retrieved December 7, 2022, from https://www.semrush.com/blog/google-algorithm-update/

Larkin, K. (2022, June 29). *What Is The Difference Between Search Queries And Keywords?* Search Engine Journal. Retrieved March 18, 2023, from

https://www.searchenginejournal.com/understanding-difference-queries-keywords/126421/#close

Leist, R. (2022, January 7). *How to Do Keyword Research for SEO: A Beginner's Guide*. HubSpot Blog. Retrieved November 30, 2022, from https://blog.hubspot.com/marketing/how-to-do-keyword-research-ht

Lyons, K. (2022, July 6). *Long-Tail Keywords: What They Are & How to Use Them for SEO*. SEMrush. Retrieved November 30, 2022, from https://www.semrush.com/blog/how-to-choose-long-tail-keywords/

Marchant, R. (2016, June 3). *Citation building the most popular link building tactic for Local SEOs*. BrightLocal. Retrieved December 18, 2022, from https://www.brightlocal.com/research/citation-building-rated-the-most-popular-link-building-tactic-for-local-seos/

MDN contributors. (2022, September 20). *First contentful paint - MDN Web Docs Glossary: Definitions of Web-related terms | MDN*. MDN Web Docs. Retrieved December 7, 2022, from https://developer.mozilla.org/en-US/docs/Glossary/First_contentful_paint

Melnick, M. (2017, September 29). *Web 101: Common HTML Elements*. Wingard. Retrieved December 8, 2022, from https://wearewingard.com/web-101-common-html-elements/

Merriam webster. (n.d.). *Competency Definition & Meaning*. Merriam-Webster. Retrieved December 29, 2022, from https://www.merriam-webster.com/dictionary/competency

Meyers, P. J. (2019, May 14). *How Often Does Google Update Its Algorithm?* Moz. Retrieved November 30, 2022, from https://moz.com/blog/how-often-does-google-update-its-algorithm

Meyers, P. J. (2019, May 14). *How Often Does Google Update Its Algorithm?* Moz. Retrieved December 28, 2022, from https://moz.com/blog/how-often-does-google-update-its-algorithm

Monaghan, M. (2022, October 27). *Website Load Time Statistics: Why Speed Matters in 2022.* Website Builder Expert. Retrieved November 30, 2022, from https://www.websitebuilderexpert.com/building-websites/website-load-time-statistics/

Moriarty, B. (2022, April 15). *Storytelling in Business: How to Create Engaging Stories | Darden Ideas to Action.* Darden Ideas to Action. Retrieved December 28, 2022, from https://ideas.darden.virginia.edu/storytelling-in-business-engaging-stories

Moz. (n.d.). *Domain Authority: What is it and how is it calculated.* Moz. Retrieved December 27, 2022, from https://moz.com/learn/seo/domain-authority

Moz. (n.d.). *Internal Links SEO Best Practices.* Moz. Retrieved December 14, 2022, from https://moz.com/learn/seo/internal-link

Moz. (n.d.). *What Are External Links? Best Practices For Building Authority*. Moz. Retrieved December 14, 2022, from https://moz.com/learn/seo/external-link

Moz. (n.d.). *What Are Keywords And Why Are They Important For SEO?* Moz. Retrieved November 30, 2022, from https://moz.com/learn/seo/what-are-keywords

Moz. (n.d.). *What Is A URL And Why Do They Matter For SEO?* Moz. Retrieved December 3, 2022, from https://moz.com/learn/seo/url

Moz. (n.d.). *What Is Conversion Rate Optimization? How To Calculate CRO*. Moz. Retrieved December 27, 2022, from https://moz.com/learn/seo/conversion-rate-optimization

Moz. (n.d.). *What Is On-Site SEO? How To Optimize A Page*. Moz. Retrieved December 12, 2022, from https://moz.com/learn/seo/on-site-seo

Mozilla. (2022, September 14). *What is JavaScript? - Learn web development | MDN*. MDN Web Docs. Retrieved December 8, 2022, from https://developer.mozilla.org/en-US/docs/Learn/JavaScript/First_steps/What_is_JavaScript

Mozilla Developer. (2022, August 29). *Link types: noopener - HTML: HyperText Markup Language | MDN*. MDN Web Docs. Retrieved

December 22, 2022, from https://developer.mozilla.org/en-US/docs/Web/HTML/Link_types/noopener

Mozilla Developer. (2022, October 30). *Functions - JavaScript | MDN.* MDN Web Docs. Retrieved December 9, 2022, from https://developer.mozilla.org/en-US/docs/Web/JavaScript/Guide/Functions

Mueller, J. (2021, August 23). *johnmu: cats are not people on Twitter: "@The_Scorpionboy No effect on SEO. Like ads, like social media. It's good to have multiple separate sources of traffic to your website, and not everything needs to have an SEO effect."* Twitter. Retrieved December 22, 2022, from https://twitter.com/JohnMu/status/1429847035319103493

Nelson, C. (n.d.). *What creators should know about Google's August 2022 helpful content update | Google Search Central Blog.* Google Developers. Retrieved December 7, 2022, from https://developers.google.com/search/blog/2022/08/helpful-content-update

Oh, S. (2021, July 14). *Case Study: Does Broken Link Building Work Today?* YouTube. Retrieved December 22, 2022, from https://www.youtube.com/watch?v=k_0jmRvK4gs

Osmani, A., & Pollard, B. (2022, October 25). *Optimize Cumulative Layout Shift*. web.dev. Retrieved December 5, 2022, from https://web.dev/optimize-cls/

Patel, N. (n.d.). *How to Boost Your SEO by Using Schema Markup*. Neil Patel. Retrieved December 5, 2022, from https://neilpatel.com/blog/get-started-using-schema/

Patrick, S. (n.d.). *Importance of Geotagging your Keywords for SEO*. SEO Hacker. Retrieved November 30, 2022, from https://seo-hacker.com/keyword-geotagging-seo/

Payne, J. (2021, August 26). *What is a 301 Redirect, and When Should You Use One?* HubSpot Blog. Retrieved December 5, 2022, from https://blog.hubspot.com/blog/tabid/6307/bid/7430/what-is-a-301-redirect-and-why-should-you-care.aspx

Pernice, K. (2017, November 12). *F-Shaped Pattern of Reading on the Web: Misunderstood, But Still Relevant (Even on Mobile)*. Nielsen Norman Group. Retrieved December 17, 2022, from https://www.nngroup.com/articles/f-shaped-pattern-reading-web-content/

Pew Research Center. (2005, January 23). *Part 1. Introduction*. Pew Research Center. Retrieved April 17, 2023, from https://www.pewresearch.org/internet/2005/01/23/part-1-introduction-8/

PluralSight. (n.d.). *JavaScript Conditionals: The Basics with Examples.* JavaScript.com. Retrieved December 9, 2022, from https://www.javascript.com/learn/conditionals

Pokorny, E. (2022, March 11). *Hreflang language codes: 2022 list and how to use them.* Weglot Translate. Retrieved December 4, 2022, from https://weglot.com/blog/hreflang-language-codes-2022-list-and-how-to-use-them/

Prater, M. (2021, June 9). *25 Google Search Statistics to Bookmark ASAP.* HubSpot Blog. Retrieved April 16, 2023, from https://blog.hubspot.com/marketing/google-search-statistics

Rankin, T. (2019, June 27). How to Optimize JavaScript and CSS and Improve Website Performance. Retrieved December 9, 2022, from https://torquemag.io/2019/06/optimize-javascript-css/

Rocket Content. (2020, September 30). *Largest Contentful Paint (LCP): what it is and how to improve it.* Rock Content. Retrieved December 5, 2022, from https://rockcontent.com/blog/largest-contentful-paint/

Search engine. (n.d.). Wikipedia. Retrieved November 30, 2022, from https://en.wikipedia.org/wiki/Search_engine

Search Engine Journal. (2018, August 2). *Which Digital Marketing*

    Channel Has the Highest ROI for Websites? [POLL]. Search

    Engine Journal. Retrieved April 16, 2023, from

    https://www.searchenginejournal.com/digital-marketing-channel-

    highest-roi/263757/#close

Searchmetrics. (n.d.). *Conversion – SEO Glossary*. Searchmetrics.

    Retrieved December 27, 2022, from

    https://www.searchmetrics.com/glossary/conversion/

Search Metrics. (2022). *Search volume - find the definition in the SEO*

    Glossary. Searchmetrics. Retrieved November 30, 2022, from

    https://www.searchmetrics.com/glossary/search-volume/

Seer interactive. (2022, March 14). *How to Use SEMRush to Identify*

    Search Trends and Competitor Insights. Seer Interactive. Retrieved

    December 28, 2022, from

    https://www.seerinteractive.com/insights/how-to-use-semrush-to-

    identify-search-trends-and-competitor-insights

SEO Keywords. (n.d.). WooRank. Retrieved November 30, 2022, from

    https://www.woorank.com/en/edu/seo-guides/what-are-keywords-

    in-seo

Sickler, J. (2021, April 30). *What is E-A-T & Why it's Important (Google,*
   E-A-T and SEO). Terakeet. Retrieved November 30, 2022, from
   https://terakeet.com/blog/what-is-eat/

Silva, C. (2022, December 12). *What Is Off-Page SEO? A Guide to Off-*
   Page SEO Strategy. Semrush. Retrieved April 8, 2023, from
   https://www.semrush.com/blog/off-page-seo/

Slawski, B., Slawski's, B., & slawski, b. (2006, February 5). *What was the*
   First Search Engine? SEO by the Sea. Retrieved December 7,
   2022, from https://www.seobythesea.com/2006/02/just-what-was-
   the-first-search-engine/

Soulo, T. (2022, May 9). *Keyword Difficulty: How to Estimate Your*
   Chances to Rank. Ahrefs. Retrieved November 30, 2022, from
   https://ahrefs.com/blog/keyword-difficulty/

Soulo, T. (2022, September 13). *Keyword Research: The Beginner's*
   Guide by Ahrefs. Ahrefs. Retrieved November 30, 2022, from
   https://ahrefs.com/blog/keyword-research/

Southern, M. G. (2020, September 15). *Google's John Mueller: Keywords*
   in Domain Name Aren't Needed. Search Engine Journal. Retrieved
   December 31, 2022, from
   https://www.searchenginejournal.com/keywords-in-domain-
   name/380912/#close

Southern, M. G. (2022, December 15). *Google E-E-A-T: How To Demonstrate First-Hand Experience*. Search Engine Journal. Retrieved January 15, 2023, from https://www.searchenginejournal.com/google-e-e-a-t-how-to-demonstrate-first-hand-experience/474446/

Spinutech. (2018, June 14). *SEO FAQ: Keyword Rankings Explained*. Spinutech. Retrieved December 27, 2022, from https://www.spinutech.com/digital-marketing/seo/analytics/seo-faq-keyword-rankings-explained/

Stanford, L. (n.d.). *US6285999B1 - Method for node ranking in a linked database*. Google Patents. Retrieved December 17, 2022, from https://patents.google.com/patent/US6285999

Stox, P. (2022, February 23). *What Are Core Web Vitals & How Can You Improve Them?* Ahrefs. Retrieved December 4, 2022, from https://ahrefs.com/blog/core-web-vitals/

Sullivan, D. (n.d.). *Evolving "nofollow" – new ways to identify the nature of links | Google Search Central Blog*. Google Developers. Retrieved December 22, 2022, from https://developers.google.com/search/blog/2019/09/evolving-nofollow-new-ways-to-identify

Sullivan, D. (2019, August 01). *What site owners should know about Google's August 2019 core update | Google Search Central Blog.* Google Developers. Retrieved November 30, 2022, from https://developers.google.com/search/blog/2019/08/core-updates

Sullivan, D. (2022, May 25). *May 2022 core update releasing for Google Search | Google Search Central Blog.* Google Developers. Retrieved November 30, 2022, from https://developers.google.com/search/blog/2022/05/may-2022-core-update

Sullivan, D. (2022, August 18). *More content by people, for people in Search.* The Keyword. Retrieved November 30, 2022, from https://blog.google/products/search/more-content-by-people-for-people-in-search/

Theuring, J. (2022, October 12). *Bing vs Google: Search Engine Comparison 2022.* Impression. Retrieved December 7, 2022, from https://www.impression.co.uk/blog/bing-differ-google/

Tutorial Republic. (n.d.). *Adding JavaScript to HTML Document.* Tutorial Republic. Retrieved December 9, 2022, from https://www.tutorialrepublic.com/javascript-tutorial/javascript-get-started.php

Tutorialspoint. (n.d.). *JavaScript - Syntax*. Tutorialspoint. Retrieved

    December 8, 2022, from

    https://www.tutorialspoint.com/javascript/javascript_syntax.htm

Tutorials Teacher. (n.d.). *JavaScript Variables (With Examples)*.

    TutorialsTeacher. Retrieved December 9, 2022, from

    https://www.tutorialsteacher.com/javascript/javascript-variable

Ugor, M. (2022, June 7). *600000 Link Outreach Emails Analyzed: Here"s*

    What Works. Authority Hacker. Retrieved December 18, 2022,

    from https://www.authorityhacker.com/link-building-outreach/

Vura, T. (n.d.). *Google Algorithm Updates: A Running Timeline of Major*

    Changes. BrightEdge. Retrieved November 30, 2022, from

    https://www.brightedge.com/blog/google-algorithm-updates-

    running-timeline-major-changes

W3school. (n.d.). *HTML Styles CSS*. W3Schools. Retrieved December 9,

    2022, from https://www.w3schools.com/html/html_css.asp

W3School. (n.d.). *HTML Tutorial*. W3Schools. Retrieved December 9,

    2022, from https://www.w3schools.com/html/default.asp

W3School. (n.d.). *JavaScript Events*. W3Schools. Retrieved December 9,

    2022, from https://www.w3schools.com/js/js_events.asp

W3School. (n.d.). *JavaScript Statements*. W3Schools. Retrieved

December 9, 2022, from

https://www.w3schools.com/js/js_statements.asp

W3school. (n.d.). *What is JavaScript*. W3Schools. Retrieved December 8,

2022, from https://www.w3schools.com/whatis/whatis_js.asp

W3Schools. (n.d.). *JavaScript Functions*. W3Schools. Retrieved March

29, 2023, from https://www.w3schools.com/js/js_functions.asp

Walden, H. (2022, April 14). *What Does the rel="noopener noreferrer"*

Tag Mean? (& Does It Affect SEO?). Elegant Themes. Retrieved

December 22, 2022, from

https://www.elegantthemes.com/blog/wordpress/rel-noopener-

noreferrer-nofollow

Wall, A. (2017). *Search Engine History*. Search Engine History.com.

Retrieved December 7, 2022, from

http://www.searchenginehistory.com/#search-work

Walton, P. (2019, June 11). *Cumulative Layout Shift (CLS)*. web.dev.

Retrieved December 5, 2022, from https://web.dev/cls/

Walton, P. (2019, November 7). *First Input Delay (FID)*. web.dev.

Retrieved December 5, 2022, from https://web.dev/fid/

Walton, P., & Pollard, B. (2022, September 27). *Optimize Largest Contentful Paint*. web.dev. Retrieved December 5, 2022, from https://web.dev/optimize-lcp/

Webfx. (n.d.). *Why Search Intent Matters for SEO (Plus 3 Optimization Tips)*. WebFX. Retrieved November 30, 2022, from https://www.webfx.com/seo/learn/why-search-intent-matters-to-seo/

What Are Title Tags? [Plus FREE Title Tag Preview Tool]. (n.d.). Moz. Retrieved December 13, 2022, from https://moz.com/learn/seo/title-tag

Wikipedia. (n.d.). *Anchor text*. Wikipedia. Retrieved December 14, 2022, from https://en.wikipedia.org/wiki/Anchor_text

Wikipedia. (n.d.). *CSS*. Wikipedia. Retrieved December 8, 2022, from https://en.wikipedia.org/wiki/CSS

Wikipedia. (n.d.). *Domain authority*. Wikipedia. Retrieved December 27, 2022, from https://en.wikipedia.org/wiki/Domain_authority

Wikipedia. (n.d.). *HTML*. Wikipedia. Retrieved December 8, 2022, from https://en.wikipedia.org/wiki/HTML

Wikipedia. (n.d.). *JumpStation*. Wikipedia. Retrieved December 7, 2022, from https://en.wikipedia.org/wiki/JumpStation

Wikipedia. (n.d.). *MSN*. Wikipedia. Retrieved December 7, 2022, from

    https://en.wikipedia.org/wiki/MSN

Wikipedia. (n.d.). *Performance indicator*. Wikipedia. Retrieved December

    24, 2022, from

    https://en.wikipedia.org/wiki/Performance_indicator

Wikipedia. (n.d.). *URL*. Wikipedia. Retrieved December 3, 2022, from

    https://en.wikipedia.org/wiki/URL

Wikipedia. (n.d.). *Web hosting service*. Wikipedia. Retrieved December 5,

    2022, from https://en.wikipedia.org/wiki/Web_hosting_service

Wikipedia. (n.d.). *World Wide Web*. Wikipedia. Retrieved December 3,

    2022, from https://en.wikipedia.org/wiki/World_Wide_Web

Wikipedia. (n.d.). *World Wide Web*. Wikipedia. Retrieved December 7,

    2022, from https://en.wikipedia.org/wiki/World_Wide_Web

Wikipedia. (n.d.). *World Wide Web Worm*. Wikipedia. Retrieved

    December 7, 2022, from

    https://en.wikipedia.org/wiki/World_Wide_Web_Worm

Wikipedia. (n.d.). *Yahoo! Search*. Wikipedia. Retrieved December 7,

    2022, from https://en.wikipedia.org/wiki/Yahoo!_Search

Woorank. (n.d.). *What is an XML Sitemap?* WooRank. Retrieved

    December 3, 2022, from https://www.woorank.com/en/edu/seo-

    guides/xml-sitemaps

Xu, L. (2018, January 10). *9 Most Common Schema Markup Types*.

Overdrive Interactive. Retrieved December 5, 2022, from

https://www.ovrdrv.com/blog/9-most-common-schema-markup-

types/

Yoast. (2021, September 22). *Long-tail keywords: why they deserve your*

focus! • Yoast. Yoast. Retrieved November 30, 2022, from

https://yoast.com/focus-on-long-tail-keywords/

Photo Credits

Amethyststudio, Support gradient icon , accessed 6 April 2023, <http://www.canva.com>

Cu-by-Design, Computer data brain , accessed 6 April 2023, <http://www.canva.com>

DAPA Images, Panda bear, accessed 6 April 2023, <http://www.canva.com>

DAPA Images, Silhouette of a rockstar playing guitars, accessed 6 April 2023, <http://www.canva.com>

deMysticwWay from Pixabay, Flag of Spain illustration , accessed 6 April 2023, <http://www.canva.com>

djvstock, Businessman climbing to success, accessed 10 April 2023, <http://www.canva.com>

Google Design Icons, Folder, Digital Image, accessed 6 November 2022, <http://www.canva.com>

Icons0.com, Check mark icon, accessed 6 April 2023, <http://www.canva.com>

Icons8, Broken phone, accessed 6 April 2023, <http://www.canva.com>

Icons8, Florida, accessed 6 April 2023, <http://www.canva.com>

Icons8, Link Digital Image, accessed 6 April 2023, <http://www.canva.com>

Icons8, Server, accessed 6 April 2023, <http://www.canva.com>

Icon54, Global SEO, Digital Image, accessed 6 November 2022, <http://www.canva.com>

inkit from Getty Image Signature, A laptop displaying search engine results, Digital Image, accessed 6 November 2022, <http://www.canva.com>

Jemastock, Coffee cup, accessed 6 April 2023, <http://www.canva.com>

Jenzon Lopez from Sketchify Education, Flat cartoon badge, Digital Image, accessed 6 April 2023, <http://www.canva.com>

Karyna Amanova, Comic speed motion lines, Digital Image, accessed 6 November 2022, <http://www.canva.com>

Leremy Gan, Fatman Icon, accessed 6 April 2023, <http://www.canva.com>

Marina2806, Search bar icon, Digital Image, accessed 6 April 2023, <http://www.canva.com>

Mohamed_hassan from Pixabay, Hummingbird icon, Digital Image, accessed 6 April 2023, <http://www.canva.com>

Olegar, King penguin icon, accessed 6 April 2023, <http://www.canva.com>

OpenClipart-Vectors from Pixabay, Computer Monitor Illustration , accessed 6 April 2023, <http://www.canva.com>

OpenClipart-Vectors from Pixabay, Vector image , accessed 6 April 2023, <http://www.canva.com>

OpenClipart-Vectors from Pixabay, Flag of France illustration , accessed 6 April 2023, <http://www.canva.com>

Puckung, Maintenance Icon, Digital Image, accessed 6 April 2022, <http://www.canva.com>

Royyan Wijaya, Bot , accessed 6 April 2023, <http://www.canva.com>

Sachin Modgekar, Open Hand, Digital Image, accessed 6 November 2022, <http://www.canva.com>.

Sergiy Tkachenko, Kent, Digital Font, accessed 6 November 2022, <http://www.canva.com>.

Sorembaddesignz, Webpage, accessed 6 April 2023, <http://www.canva.com>

Wibke from Pixabay, Flag of France illustration , accessed 6 April 2023, <http://www.canva.com>

4Zer, Cardboardbox, accessed 6 April 2023, <http://www.canva.com>

About the Author

Roggie (Raj) Clark, is an 8 year SEO professional and owner of the SEO agency; *Bounce Rank.* Prior to joining the SEO industry, Raj was a web developer and schoolteacher. It was through creating his own websites, and wanting a career change from teaching, that Raj stumbled across the world of SEO.

Since joining the field nearly, a decade ago, Raj has worked on a wide range of campaigns, from eCommerce, to B2B, to Healthcare, for enterprise companies and marketing agencies in the United States.

He is regarded as an expert, and guru by his colleagues, and the SEO industry. Raj currently lives in Maryland with his sister and niece.

Consulting or Coaching Services

I know that from reading this book, it simply may not be enough information for you or you may require more personalized support with your unique business situation.

So because of that, I'm offering the opportunity to receive consulting or coaching from me on SEO. I can offer support with:

- Creating SOPs (Standard Operating Procedures)
- Creating SEO strategies
- SEO implementation
- Content suggestions
- Technical audits
- Web design/migrations
- Competitor analysis
- Keyword research
- SEO career coaching

If you are interested in any of these services, or would like to request more information, for a specific need you may have.

Please email me at **bouncerankseo@gmail.com**. In your email, please include the following information:

- Your name
- The business you represent (if applicable)
- Team size (if applicable)
- The type of service you would like to receive
- The length of service needed
- Any other important information I should know

My administrative assistant will email you back within 24 - 48 hours with rates, and an information sheet for you to review. Thank you so much for your time and interest.

Thank you for reading!

Good luck on your SEO journey.

- Raj

www.ingramcontent.com/pod-product-compliance
Lightning Source LLC
Chambersburg PA
CBHW060144060326
40690CB00018B/3974